Every vote is a Prayer

Also edited by Cathy Cambron

The Way Women Are: Transformative Opinions and Dissents of Justice Ruth Bader Ginsburg

Let the Law Catch Up: Thurgood Marshall in His Own Words

Every vote is a *Prayer*

Get Inspired, Get Registered, Get Educated, and Vote!

Edited by Cathy Cambron

Welcome Rain Publishers
New York

Every Vote Is a Prayer

Sources for the quotations throughout the book appear on the book page for *Every Vote Is a Prayer* at welcomerain.com.

Designed by Laura Smyth, Smythtype Design

Cover photos: (top) Photo in the National Woman's Party Records (I:159), Library of Congress; (bottom) Civil rights march on Washington, D.C. (1963) Library of Congress

10 9 8 7 6 5 4 3 2 1

Library of Congress Cataloging in Publication data is available from the publisher.

Printed in the USA

ISBN: 978-1-56649-431-1 (pbk)
ISBN: 978-1-56649-432-8 (hc)

CONTENTS

INTRODUCTION

How You Can Help Fix the United States

I think a vote is a kind of prayer about the world we desire for ourselves and our children. And our prayers are stronger when we pray together.
—Rev. Raphael Warnock, U.S. senator from Georgia

If I choose not to speak out of fear, then there's no one that my silence is standing for. And so I came to realize that I cannot stand standing to the side, standing silent. I must find the strength to speak up.... Poetry is always at the pulse of the most dangerous and most daring questions that a nation or a world might face. What path do we stand on as a people, and what future as a people do we stand for?
—Amanda Gorman, poet

☆

Politics. Many Americans these days associate the word with divisiveness, anger, polarization, and chaos. A 2023 survey found that nearly two-thirds of adults say they always or often feel exhausted when they think about politics; only 10 percent reported often feeling hopeful.

But the intense political polarization that is getting on Americans' collective last nerve does have a silver lining: after decades of stagnant participation, more of us are showing up to vote in elections lately. Two-thirds of the eligible voters turned out to vote in the hotly contested 2020 presidential election, the highest rate for a national election in 120 years. The 2018 and 2022 midterms also saw historically high rates of participation.

Nevertheless, certain groups vote much more often than others. Notably, younger people tend to make up much more of the nonvoter population: 64 percent of the nonvoters in the 2022 election were under the age of 50.

There are lots of reasons people don't vote. They may not follow the news or even know how to vote; they may be cynical about government and politicians; they may feel that their vote doesn't count. It may be inconvenient and even difficult to vote. If options such as early voting and absentee voting aren't available, it may be impossible for some to get off work, arrange for transportation, or juggle childcare, especially if lines are long at the voting location.

This book is a declaration that you should try your hardest to vote anyway. It's a compendium of voices reflecting the hurdles that Black people, women, Native Americans, and young people of previous generations overcame so that we would have access to the expression of our right to self-government. It's a plea for us all to become involved so that our government can reflect the voices of us all. It's an acknowledgment that elections are messy, complicated, frustrating, and divisive and yet represent the most powerful way that ordinary citizens can have an effect on our country's future.

Participating in elections is a way of being part of the community. It's a way of holding politicians accountable, not just passively disapproving of them. Voting is a way to honor those who came before us, whose dreams and hopes we embody. And it's a way to reaffirm that your voice matters—and that the future we decide on together matters, too.

☆

The only way we can begin to make things better is to choose leaders who are willing to face these issues and find ways to work through them.

—Taylor Swift, singer, songwriter

You have to turn people on before you can turn them out.

—Al Sharpton, minister and civil rights activist

Our lives begin to end the day we become silent about things that matter.

—Martin Luther King, Jr., minister and civil rights leader

I vote for all the people who made a way—out of no way—so that I might live in a world of choices. I vote for those who marched and prayed and sacrificed and withstood humiliations and disrespect and devastation just trying to cast a ballot. I vote for those who died carrying the dream that one day their vote would be counted and could matter. I vote for the shoulders I stand on.

—Oprah Winfrey, television host, producer, actor, author

Hope Is the Thing with Feathers—Emily Dickinson

Dickinson's poem was published in 1891.

Hope is the thing with feathers
That perches in the soul,
And sings the tune without the words,
And never stops at all,

And sweetest in the gale is heard;
And sore must be the storm
That could abash the little bird
That kept so many warm.

I've heard it in the chillest land,
And on the strangest sea;
Yet, never, in extremity,
It asked a crumb of me.

☆

A Brief History of U.S. Voting

Voting in the Early Years

In the 1780s, when the United States was new, voting varied widely from locality to locality. The requirement that voters be white male property owners, a carryover from the days of British governance, was largely but not consistently followed; for example, from 1776 to 1807, women who owned property and free Black men could vote in New Jersey.

The U.S. Constitution, ratified with the Bill of Rights by 1791, reflected the competing interests of states with very different economies and cultures. The Constitution's Three-Fifths Compromise allowed southern states, with more than half a million enslaved inhabitants, to count each one of them as three-fifths of a person for purposes of deciding how many representatives each state would have in Congress, as well as how many electors would represent the state in the

Electoral College, the body that selects the U.S. president. The Constitution largely leaves the states in charge of deciding on the time, place, and manner of electing representatives to Congress and to the Electoral College.

☆

> The codification of racism and disenfranchisement is a feature of our lawmaking—not an oversight. And the original sin of the U.S. Constitution began by identifying Blacks in America as three-fifths human: counting black bodies as property and their souls as nonexistent.
>
> —Stacey Abrams, lawyer and former Georgia state representative

The Electoral College

The states historically selected electors for the Electoral College in various ways; they were appointed by state legislatures in some states and chosen by voters in others, by district or statewide elections. Today, the political parties in each state select a slate of electors; once the votes are cast in the presidential election, the electors for the winning candidate in the state are appointed to the Electoral College. The candidate for president who receives the majority of electors' votes (270 out of 538) then wins the election, regardless of who wins the "popular vote," or the most overall votes nationally.

Currently, most states follow a winner-takes-all-electors rule; only two states, Nebraska and Maine, provide for proportional representation in the Electoral College based on the percentage of the vote received by each candidate for president. The winner-takes-all rule followed by all the other states means that in the presidential election, some voters have more say in the outcome: namely, those who live in more rural states and in "swing" states that have fairly equal numbers of voters supporting each of the two major political parties.

The National Popular Vote agreement, with sixteen states and the District of Columbia signing on to date, would change the way electors are appointed so that the result in the Electoral College would mirror the outcome of the popular vote. About 65 percent of Americans reportedly favor having the popular vote rather than the Electoral College determine who will be president.

The only way to make progress is if every single American is empowered to vote—and those who have historically been drawn out of our democracy are able to make their voices heard so that this country can live up to its full promise and potential.
—Beto O'Rourke, former U.S. representative from Texas

Everyone needs to have their voices heard and we can do that by VOTING. We will not let voter suppression stop us!
—Selena Gomez, actor, singer

The Fifteenth Amendment and the Voting Rights Act

In the years leading up to the Civil War, the states largely expanded voting rights for white men, dropping the requirement of owning property. At the same time, most of the states that had allowed voting by free Black men changed their laws to restrict voting to white men only. For example, in 1838, delegates at Pennsylvania's constitutional convention added a clause to the state constitution limiting voting to whites, over the protests of free Black voters in the state (see Robert Purvis speech in chapter 3).

After slavery was abolished in the United States with President Abraham Lincoln's Emancipation Proclamation on January 1, 1863, and with the end of the Civil War in 1865, the issue of whether formerly enslaved people would be permitted to vote became a pressing one. The Fifteenth Amendment to the U.S. Constitution, proposed in 1869 and ratified in 1870, guaranteed the right to vote to the formerly enslaved—but crucially, federal enforcement of that right ceased entirely with the end of postwar Reconstruction in 1877. Decisions of the Supreme Court in the *Slaughter-House Cases* (1873) and *Plessy v. Ferguson* (1896) curtailed the power of the federal government to protect Black people's constitutional rights and enshrined as constitutional the comprehensive system of racial segregation known as Jim Crow. Black Americans, particularly in the South, were prevented from voting by a wide variety of means—from violence and intimidation to poll taxes and "literacy tests"—or were simply refused a ballot by officials who knew there would be no consequences for the refusal.

It wasn't until nearly one hundred years after the Civil War that Black Americans' constitutional rights began to be respected, as a result of lawsuits, marches, sit-ins, and other forms of pressure from participants in the civil rights movement—many of whom were beaten, jailed, and even killed for their efforts. The Supreme Court overturned *Plessy v. Ferguson* and declared racial segregation in public schools unconstitutional in 1954, in *Brown v. Board of Education of Topeka*. A turning point for voting rights came with "Bloody Sunday," March 7, 1965, when John Lewis, who was later elected to Congress, led more than six hundred unarmed, peaceful civil rights marchers across the Edmund Pettus Bridge in Selma, Alabama—where state troopers tear-gassed the protesters and attacked them with clubs, bullwhips, and dogs as television cameras rolled. Within days, President Lyndon B. Johnson began pushing through Congress the Voting Rights Act of 1965, which brought the power of the federal government to bear in enforcing voting rights throughout the states.

The Voting Rights Act was readopted and strengthened in 1970, 1975, 1982, and 2006. More recently, however, the Supreme Court, in *Shelby County v. Holder* (2013), limited the Act by striking as unconstitutional the section that required some states to clear with the federal government any planned changes in voting laws.

☆

Casting a ballot is a great privilege—hard won by our ancestors. Please vote—you owe it to yourself and to the memory of those who came before.

—Condoleezza Rice, former U.S. secretary of state

The vote is precious, it is almost sacred. It is the most powerful nonviolent tool we have in a democratic society. And we have to use it.

—John Lewis, former U.S. representative from Georgia

The Nineteenth Amendment

American women began in an organized way to seek equal rights with men at the Seneca Falls Convention in New York in 1848. Many of the women who attended this convention had already been active in the abolitionist movement to end slavery. Renowned orator Frederick Douglass, the only Black attendee at the convention, argued in favor of including among the convention's resolutions for future action one demanding women's suffrage, and he remained an eloquent advocate of votes for women throughout his life.

For their part, two of the most prominent leaders of the women's rights movement during this time, Susan B. Anthony and Elizabeth Cady Stanton, opposed the Fifteenth Amendment of 1870 because they believed it was wrong for Black people to win the right to vote before women did. Other leading advocates for women's rights, such as Lucretia Mott, were dedicated to achieving equal rights for both Black Americans and women.

Anthony and Stanton toured the nation giving talks on women's suffrage, and they organized the National Woman Suffrage Association to urge passage of a constitutional amendment guaranteeing women's right to vote. In 1872, Anthony was arrested and fined for voting; one of her most famous speeches was prompted by the incident.

These early leaders passed the torch to others, including Alice Paul, a militant suffragist and hunger striker who authored the original Equal Rights Amendment, and Carrie Chapman Catt, who took over leadership of what was by then called the National American Woman Suffrage Association. Catt devised a plan to coordinate suffrage drives in the various states with pressure for a constitutional amendment guaranteeing votes for women. Women were able to vote in a number of states and territories before 1920, including Wyoming, Utah, Colorado, Idaho, Washington, California, Oregon, Montana, Arizona, Kansas, Alaska, Illinois, North Dakota, Indiana, Nebraska, Michigan, Arkansas, New York, South Dakota, and Oklahoma. But it wasn't until the United States became embroiled in World War I that President Woodrow Wilson, recognizing the importance of women to the war effort, was persuaded to support a constitutional amendment guaranteeing votes for women nationwide. After he announced his support in a 1918 speech to Congress, the Nineteenth Amendment was passed and ratified within two years. Carrie Chapman Catt then founded the League of Women Voters to assist women in using their newly acquired voting rights.

☆

There will never be a new world order until women are a part of it.
—Alice Paul, suffragist and author of the original Equal Rights Amendment

The best way to follow in the footsteps of the women who fought for our right to vote is to use the power of our voices. They saw that our country wasn't perfect. Yet they embraced America instead of rejecting it, and they put in the hard work to fix it. Every time we vote, we honor them.

—Nikki Haley, former U.S. ambassador to the United Nations

The Twenty-Sixth Amendment

War also played a role in lowering the voting age from 21 to 18. In 1942, as World War II raged, Congress lowered the draft age from 21 to 18. With young men who were not old enough to vote being sent overseas to fight and die for the United States, the slogan "old enough to fight, old enough to vote" became a rallying cry for youth voting. Many people, from former First Lady Eleanor Roosevelt to President Dwight D. Eisenhower, endorsed the idea from then on, but it really gained traction during the Vietnam War, as youth disaffection with the draft and an unpopular war prompted Congress to act. After the Supreme Court in 1970 made it clear that a constitutional amendment would be required to lower the voting age, Congress acted quickly to pass the Twenty-Sixth Amendment, which was ratified by the states more rapidly than any other constitutional amendment before or since and became law in 1971.

☆

By 2024, Millennials and Gen Z voters will outnumber voters who are Baby Boomers and older, 45/25. We are beginning to see the political impacts of that generational shift.

—Alexandria Ocasio-Cortez, U.S. representative from New York

Native Americans and Voting

Self-government was practiced by Native Americans long before the United States came into being, but it took many years for Native Americans to obtain the right to vote in U.S. elections. Native Americans were not admitted to full U.S. citizenship until the passage of the Snyder Act in 1924, and even after that date, some states still restricted Native voting for several decades. With the passage of the Voting Rights Act of

1965 and subsequent legislation, Native Americans nationwide finally were empowered once again to exercise their right to govern themselves.

☆

Everyone wants a place where they feel safe...where we know we can practice our ways and not be jailed or censored or anything.... People are really looking for connection and trust...leaders who are trusted because they have a history of compassion, of knowledge, and they're willing to work across any kind of political lines. Those are real leaders.

—Joy Harjo, the first Native American U.S. poet laureate

Democracy and Elections

The events of the second and third decades of the twenty-first century have led many to doubt whether the American democracy is durable. While liberals tend to seek to make voting more accessible and convenient, conservatives raise concerns about oversight, fraud, and manipulation of voting machines. The news around Election Day concerns not just the candidates and the issues, but struggles over voting rights; accusations, mainly unfounded, of voting fraud; intimidation of election workers; and disputes about options for voting. After many years of peaceful transfers of power following presidential elections, more recently a reluctance to concede defeat has taken the form of a "Big Lie" about election theft, which has led to an upsurge in political violence in the United States, including the storming of the U.S. Capitol on January 6, 2021.

In this troubled landscape, your participation is more important than ever. When we all take part in elections and see for ourselves how voting is done, we're less likely to be swayed by baseless rumors that election machines are all rigged and that most election workers can't be trusted. By doing your own research (see chapter 7) and believing the evidence rather than relying on politicians' assertions, you'll be better able to make choices that are aligned with your values.

Elected officials who believe their own political survival is more important than anything else threaten the survival of our republic, no matter what they tell themselves to justify their cowardice.
—Liz Cheney, former U.S. representative from Wyoming

Most importantly, the American people, no matter what their political persuasion, must make it clear that American democracy will not be destroyed.
—Bernie Sanders, U.S. senator from Vermont

A Note About Third Parties

Understandably, many of us are frustrated by the tight grip that the Democratic and Republican Parties maintain over the process of electing the U.S. president; we might prefer to vote for a candidate who more accurately reflects our viewpoint, rather than feeling doomed to continually vote for the "lesser of two evils." But third-party presidential candidates present a dilemma. Although these candidates are unlikely to win the election themselves, they tend to draw votes away from the major-party candidate closest to them politically, benefiting the *other* major-party candidate—who may actually be the *least* appealing option for the third-party voter. It can feel momentarily satisfying to pick exactly what you want off the menu of choices on the ballot, but you may end up being served the dish you least wanted.

☆

A vote is not a Valentine; it's a chess move.
—Rebecca Solnit, writer

I learned long ago that winning doesn't always mean you get the prize. Sometimes you get progress, and that counts.
–Stacey Abrams, lawyer and former Georgia state representative

---

For further information: Rock the Vote offers "Democracy Explainers," with succinct explanations of topics related to voting in the United States. https://rockthevote.org/explainers/

The Pew Research Center is a good source for data on voter participation: pewresearch.org

To further explore the history of voting, see Allan J. Lichtman, *The Embattled Vote in America: From the Founding to the Present* (Cambridge, MA: Harvard University Press, 2018), and Erin Geiger Smith, *Thank You for Voting: The Maddening, Enlightening, Inspiring Truth About Voting in America* (New York: Harper, 2020).

CHAPTER 1
Get It Done: Register and Make a Plan to Vote

Many have fought for and even lost their lives to end segregation, to win the right to vote. It disappoints me to now have to cajole people to register and to vote.
—Jesse Jackson, minister and civil rights activist

Ask yourself: Do you know where your polling place is? Do you know when your primary elections are held? Do you know how to request a mail-in ballot? Who are the incumbents and candidates at every level of government—not just president but state representative and city council and prosecutor and sheriff?
—Michelle Obama, former First Lady

☆

Take the First Step

The first step to making sure you can vote is to figure out whether you're eligible to vote and whether you will be required to show identification.

Are You Eligible to Vote?

The following are the main requirements for you to be eligible to register and vote:

★ U.S. citizenship: You must be a United States citizen, either by birth or through naturalization. Non-citizens, including permanent legal residents, cannot vote in federal elections.

★ Age requirement: You must be at least 18 years old on or before Election Day. Some states allow pre-registration before age 18 if you will be 18 by the next election.

★ State residency: You must meet the residency requirements of the state where you wish to vote. Each state has its own rules regarding residency.

★ Voter registration: Unless you live in North Dakota, which does not require voter registration, you must be registered to vote by your state's registration deadline. Registration rules vary by state.

★ No felony convictions (in some states): Some states restrict voting rights for those convicted of certain felonies, at least temporarily. The laws vary across states.

Resources listed in the next section can help you figure out if you are eligible to vote and whether you will need an ID.

☆

Even if [people] are in jail paying their price to society, that should not take away their inherent American right to participate in our democracy.
—Bernie Sanders, U.S. senator from Vermont

If you're voting for the first time, or you're still not sure if you even wanna vote—because you think your voice won't make an impact, or you don't trust the process, or it all seems just like a headache... all I can say is, we really need you.
–Justin Timberlake, singer and producer

Register and Make a Plan

Timing is everything. You may have to register as long as a month before Election Day, depending on where you live and how you register. In North Carolina, for example, you have to register at least 25 days before Election Day. The National Voter Registration Act of 1993 requires that states set their voter registration deadlines for federal elections no more than 30 days before an election.

You can find out whether you're registered to vote online. Resources listed here let you check, and then begin the registration process if you need to. They also offer information about requesting an absentee ballot, whether early voting is available before Election Day, and the polling place where you will go to vote on Election Day—so you can make a plan to vote.

- ⋆ Vote.gov has tools to help you register to vote, find voter registration deadlines, register after you've moved, change your political party affiliation, and more. https://vote.gov/

- ⋆ USA.gov has a voting and elections page with links for registering to vote, voting options (absentee, early), voter guides and sample ballots, and more. https://www.usa.gov/voting-and-elections

- ⋆ Vote.org is a nonpartisan nonprofit with a website that provides "everything you need to vote," allowing you to check your registration, start the voter registration process, see what's on your ballot, request an absentee ballot, or get election reminders. https://www.vote.org/

- ⋆ Vote411.org, a project of the League of Women Voters, provides ways for you to check your registration, start the registration process, find out what's on your local ballot, and find your polling place. The website also lists phone numbers to call in the event of election day problems and provides an interactive map to allow you to check voting options in your state. https://www.vote411.org/

- ⋆ All In to Vote, a nonpartisan initiative aimed at increasing participation by college students, offers a way to check your voter registration, answers to frequently asked questions about voting, and an opportunity to take a pledge to vote: https://allintovote.org/

- ⋆ Rock the Vote offers a page on voting information with "all the information you need to vote in your state." Selecting your state on an interactive map allows see your voting options, learn about voter registration deadlines, and begin the registration process. https://www.rockthevote.org/how-to-vote/

- ⋆ Headcount, which has partnered with artists such as Ariana Grande, Dave Matthews, Harry Styles, David Byrne, and Billie Eilish, offers links on its website to check your registration and register to vote. Headcount also has a presence at concerts and festivals—"anywhere we can translate the power of music and culture into real action." https://www.headcount.org/

★ When We All Vote is a national, nonpartisan initiative "on a mission to change the culture around voting and to increase participation in each and every election by helping to close the race and age gap." Created by Michelle Obama, the initiative works to educate people about the voting process and help them get registered to vote. The website offers a Voter Resources Hub with links to help you get ready to vote. https://whenweallvote.org/

★ Restore Your Vote, a project of Campaign Legal Center, offers an anonymous way to determine whether as a convicted felon you are eligible to vote in your state, and if not, whether you are eligible to go through the process of restoring your vote. https://campaignlegal.org/restoreyourvote

★ VoteRiders.org offers an interactive map with up-to-date information about state voter ID laws. The organization helps people without identification to secure the required ID so that they can vote. https://www.voteriders.org/

★ Transform the Vote offers resources to help transgender people feel empowered to vote even if the gender on their ID does not match their gender identity. https://transformthevote.org/voting

Primaries and Party Affiliation

Your state may offer you the opportunity when you're registering to declare a political party affiliation, such as Democrat or Republican. Declaring a political party affiliation doesn't require you to vote for the party in the general election, but it may restrict you to that party's ballot in primaries, which determine candidates in the general election. The National Conference of State Legislatures has a "State Primary Election Types" page that lists whether your state's primary elections are "open," allowing voters to "cross party lines" and request whatever ballot they want; "closed," restricting voters to their own party's ballot; or something in between: https://www.ncsl.org/elections-and-campaigns/state-primary-election-types

☆

Everyone must determine, how do I need to vote? What do I need to do? And now is the time to do it.... Figure it out and figure it out today. Because this is the most important thing that any American ever does, is decide the fate of our country.

—Loretta Lynch, former U.S. attorney general

There's no greater responsibility than being in control of your future and your future starts now!... No procrastinating, don't let the discouragement take you off course, that's not how my people or my generation will go down.... This is the loudest way to make your voice heard!

—Rihanna, singer, songwriter, actor, entrepreneur

Review a Sample Ballot

You'll want to make sure you know about the issues and candidates on your ballot. It isn't just about who you want to be president; it's about who's going to be your local sheriff, on your school board, running your county or city government, spending your taxes. If we want government to be better, focusing on the levels closest to our day-to-day lives may be the best place to start.

Reviewing a sample ballot ahead of time gives you an opportunity to evaluate candidates' qualifications and the pros and cons of the issues before making a decision. A completed sample ballot can also help speed things up in the voting booth.

★ The League of Women Voters has a long history of producing nonpartisan guides in which candidates answer questions about their qualifications and stands on the issues. Vote411.org has an interactive tool for you to view the responses of candidates on your ballot and make selections that you can save, so you can plan how you'll mark your ballot when you're in the voting booth. https://www.vote411.org/

★ Ballotpedia, a "digital encyclopedia of American politics," provides detailed, neutral information on elections and their outcomes, as well as politics and policies. The website's main page features a sample ballot lookup tool: you enter your address, and the tool shows you your ballot. https://ballotpedia.org/Main_Page

☆

Your vote might make the difference. Don't fool around with this—get the information you need to vote in this election.... As Rev. King wrote, "All progress is precarious." So don't sit on the sidelines. Don't hesitate. Don't have any regrets. Vote.

—Maya Angelou, poet and activist

With what is going on in our country, we need to get out to the polls and vote for what we believe in. Not showing up is not an option.

—Billie Eilish, singer, songwriter

CHAPTER 2
Your Vote Matters

Bad politicians are elected by good people who don't vote.
—Editorial Board, *Des Moines Register*

Not voting is not a protest. It is a surrender.
—Keith Ellison, Minnesota attorney general and former U.S. representative

Election Day, November, 1884—Walt Whitman

Whitman was a poet and essayist.

If I should need to name, O Western World, your powerfulest scene and show,
'Twould not be you, Niagara—nor you, ye limitless prairies—nor your huge rifts of canyons, Colorado,
Nor you, Yosemite—nor Yellowstone, with all its spasmic geyser-loops ascending to the skies, appearing and disappearing,
Nor Oregon's white cones—nor Huron's belt of mighty lakes—nor Mississippi's stream:
—This seething hemisphere's humanity, as now, I'd name—the still small voice vibrating—America's choosing day,
(The heart of it not in the chosen—the act itself the main, the quadriennial choosing,)
The stretch of North and South arous'd—sea-board and inland—Texas to Maine—the Prairie States—Vermont, Virginia, California,
The final ballot-shower from East to West—the paradox and conflict,
The countless snow-flakes falling—(a swordless conflict,
Yet more than all Rome's wars of old, or modern Napoleon's:) the peaceful choice of all,
Or good or ill humanity—welcoming the darker odds, the dross:
—Foams and ferments the wine? it serves to purify—while the heart pants, life glows:
These stormy gusts and winds waft precious ships,
Swell'd Washington's, Jefferson's, Lincoln's sails.

I vote because I love my country. From my friends and family members who live here, to my neighbors and millions of people I don't know, I love the citizens here.... I want to know that whatever the outcome is, we raised our voices and spoke up for what we wanted.

—Demi Lovato, singer, actor

We must refuse to accept the narrative that says our nation is divided between red and blue.

—William Barber II, minister and social activist

Our Sacred Right and Duty—Franklin D. Roosevelt

Roosevelt was the U.S. president, 1933–1945.

Radio Address from the White House, October 5, 1944

My fellow Americans:

I am speaking to you tonight from the White House. I am speaking particularly on behalf of those Americans who, regardless of party—I hope you will remember that—very much hope that there will be recorded a large registration and a large vote this fall....

Nobody will ever deprive the American people of the right to vote except the American people themselves—and the only way they could do that is by not voting at all.

The continuing health and vigor of our democratic system depends on the public spirit and devotion of its citizens which find expression in the ballot box.

Every man and every woman in this Nation—regardless of party—who have the right to register and to vote, and the opportunity to register and to vote, have also the sacred obligation to register and to vote. For the free and secret ballot is the real keystone of our American Constitutional system.

....When the American people want a change of Government—even when they merely want "new faces"—they can raise the old electioneering battle cry of "throw the rascals out."...

The right to vote must be open to our citizens irrespective of race, color, or creed—without tax or artificial restriction of any kind. The

"Radio Address from the White House, October 5, 1944," *American Presidency Project*, University of California, Santa Barbara, https://www.presidency.ucsb.edu/documents/radio-address-from-the-white-house.

sooner we get to that basis of political equality, the better it will be for the country as a whole....

The full and free exercise of our sacred right and duty to vote is more important in the long run than the personal hopes or ambitions of any candidate for any office in the land.

☆

"Do not think your single vote does not matter much. The rain that refreshes the parched ground is made up of single drops."
That is why I vote.
—Meghan Markle, Duchess of Sussex

You may be pretty or plain, heavy or thin, gay or straight, poor or rich. But remember this: In an election, every voice is equally powerful—don't underestimate your vote. Voting is the great equalizer.
—Maya Angelou, poet and activist

A Handful of Ballots—Ronald Reagan

Reagan was the U.S. president, 1981–1989.

Radio Address to the Nation on Voter Participation, October 18, 1986

My fellow Americans:

...Well, in just a few weeks, we Americans are once again going to show the world the one thing that, more than any other, is the source of our strength. We'll go to the polls, and as a free people, we'll vote. This year we'll be casting ballots in many States for Senators, Governors, and other officials; and everywhere we'll be voting for a new House of Representatives. But just as important as how we vote is that we vote. Every vote cast on election day means that we the people have taken a hand in shaping our nation's future. Every time we vote we're grabbing a hold of a lifeline that's 3,000 miles long and more than two centuries old and, with millions of others, helping to pull America forward into the future. Yes, every time we vote we're standing up, side by side, with the Founding Fathers, with the men of Valley Forge, with patriots and

---

"Radio Address to the Nation on Voter Participation, October 18, 1986," Ronald Reagan Presidential Library and Museum, https://www.reaganlibrary.gov/archives/speech/radio-address-nation-voter-participation.

pioneers throughout our history, with all those who dedicated their lives to making this a nation of the people, by the people, and for the people. Every time we vote we help to make America stronger.

I'm sure you've heard friends say, "Oh, my vote won't matter." Well, the next time someone says that to you, I hope you'll remember that time and again, over the years, elections have turned on a handful of ballots.... But even when elections aren't that close, your ballot counts, because in voting, you're accepting your part in the greatest decision-making body the world has ever known, the American electorate. And as someone who's stayed up late on many election nights waiting to hear how the American people had decided, I can tell you that from where I sit—whether elections are close or not—every vote is important.

A little more than two years ago, I walked along a beach in France where American and other forces first landed in 1944 to begin their crusade in Europe. Those Americans fought, and many of them died, for the freedom that we cherish today. Every one of them knew, and we must never forget, that freedom is never more than one generation away from extinction. They knew that freedom is something that we all must join together to preserve, protect, and defend. And our first line of defense is not our weapons or our military, but our right to decide who governs us. That's a right the soldiers who fought against our men at Normandy didn't have....

Freedom is never more than one generation away from extinction.

I've visited our men and women in uniform all over the world. It's the part of this job I like best. They're some of the best we've ever had. And if you're one of them, let me say to you that helping to protect America includes helping to decide America's future, and that begins with voting. I've also visited with many young people around our country. Nothing could be more inspiring than to hear them talk about the future. And yet I've found that too many of them don't vote. If you're one of our nation's young people, I hope you'll remember that America needs your optimism, your patriotism and idealism, your thirst for opportunity in shaping the decisions of the years to come. Those decisions are going to shape your life, too. And they're too important for you to give up any part of your role in making them. So, please vote....

Voting is a precious right that for two centuries Americans have fought and died to protect. Let's all honor that sacrifice this election day. Whether you're Republican, Democrat, or Independent, . . . show that you care about America's future and get out and vote.

☆

By all means stay home if you want, but don't bullshit yourself that you're not voting. In reality, there is no such thing as not voting: you either vote by voting, or you vote by staying home and tacitly doubling the value of some Diehard's vote.

—David Foster Wallace, author

I VOTED!!!! Did you?!?!

—Kim Kardashian, socialite and media personality

Just Vote. It's Math.—Barack Obama

Obama was the U.S. president, 2009–2017.

Remarks at Howard University Commencement Ceremony,
Howard University, Washington, D.C., May 7, 2016

THE PRESIDENT: Thank you! Hello, Howard! (Applause.) H-U!

AUDIENCE: You know!

THE PRESIDENT: H-U!

AUDIENCE: You know!

THE PRESIDENT: (Laughter.) Thank you so much, everybody. Please, please, have a seat.

. . . You have to go through life with more than just passion for change; you need a strategy. I'll repeat that. I want you to have passion, but you have to have a strategy. Not just awareness, but action. Not just hashtags, but votes.

You see, change requires more than righteous anger. It requires a program, and it requires organizing. At the 1964 Democratic Convention, Fannie Lou Hamer—all five-feet-four inches tall—gave a fiery speech on the national stage. But then she went back home to

---

"Remarks by the President at Howard University Commencement Ceremony," Office of the Press Secretary, White House, May 7, 2016, https://obamawhitehouse.archives.gov/the-press-office/2016/05/07/remarks-president-howard-university-commencement-ceremony.

Mississippi and organized cotton pickers. And she didn't have the tools and technology where you can whip up a movement in minutes. She had to go door to door. And I'm so proud of the new guard of Black civil rights leaders who understand this. It's thanks in large part to the activism of young people like many of you, from Black Twitter to Black Lives Matter, that America's eyes have been opened—white, Black, Democrat, Republican—to the real problems, for example, in our criminal justice system.

It's math. If you have more votes than the other guy, you get to do what you want.

But to bring about structural change, lasting change, awareness is not enough. It requires changes in law, changes in custom. If you care about mass incarceration, let me ask you: How are you pressuring members of Congress to pass the criminal justice reform bill now pending before them? (Applause.) If you care about better policing, do you know who your district attorney is? Do you know who your state's attorney general is? Do you know the difference? Do you know who appoints the police chief and who writes the police training manual? Find out who they are, what their responsibilities are. Mobilize the community, present them with a plan, work with them to bring about change, hold them accountable if they do not deliver. Passion is vital, but you've got to have a strategy.

And your plan better include voting—not just some of the time, but all the time. (Applause.) It is absolutely true that fifty years after the Voting Rights Act, there are still too many barriers in this country to vote. There are too many people trying to erect new barriers to voting. This is the only advanced democracy on Earth that goes out of its way to make it difficult for people to vote. And there's a reason for that. There's a legacy to that.

But let me say this: Even if we dismantled every barrier to voting, that alone would not change the fact that America has some of the lowest voting rates in the free world.... People try to make this political thing really complicated. Like, what kind of reforms do we need? And how do we need to do that? You know what, just vote. It's math. If you have more votes than the other guy, you get to do what you want. (Laughter.) It's not that complicated.

And you don't have excuses. You don't have to guess the number of jellybeans in a jar or bubbles on a bar of soap to register to vote. You don't have to risk your life to cast a ballot. Other people already did that for you. (Applause.) Your grandparents, your great grandparents might be here today if they were working on it. What's your excuse? When we don't vote, we give away our power, disenfranchise ourselves—right when we need to use the power that we have; right when we need your power to stop others from taking away the vote and rights of those more vulnerable than you are—the elderly and the poor, the formerly incarcerated trying to earn their second chance.

So you've got to vote all the time, not just when it's cool, not just when it's time to elect a President, not just when you're inspired. It's your duty. When it's time to elect a member of Congress or a city councilman, or a school board member, or a sheriff. That's how we change our politics—by electing people at every level who are representative of and accountable to us. It is not that complicated. Don't make it complicated.

And finally, change requires more than just speaking out—it requires listening, as well. In particular, it requires listening to those with whom you disagree, and being prepared to compromise.... You need allies in a democracy. That's just the way it is. It can be frustrating and it can be slow. But history teaches us that the alternative to democracy is always worse. That's not just true in this country. It's not a black or white thing. Go to any country where the give and take of democracy has been repealed by one-party rule, and I will show you a country that does not work.

So you've got to vote all the time, not just when it's cool, not just when it's time to elect a President, not just when you're inspired.

And democracy requires compromise, even when you are 100 percent right. This is hard to explain sometimes. You can be completely right, and you still are going to have to engage folks who disagree with you. If you think that the only way forward is to be as uncompromising as possible, you will feel good about yourself, you will enjoy a certain moral purity, but you're not going to get what you want. And if you don't get what you want long enough, you will eventually think the whole system is rigged. And that will lead to more cynicism, and less participation, and a downward spiral of more injustice and more anger and more despair. And that's never been the source of our progress. That's how we cheat ourselves of progress.

We remember Dr. King's soaring oratory, the power of his letter from a Birmingham jail, the marches he led. But he also sat down with President Johnson in the Oval Office to try and get a Civil Rights Act and a Voting Rights Act passed. And those two seminal bills were not perfect—just like the Emancipation Proclamation was a war document as much as it was some clarion call for freedom. Those mileposts of our progress were not perfect. They did not make up for centuries of slavery or Jim Crow or eliminate racism or provide for 40 acres and a mule. But they made things better. And you know what, I will take better every time. I always tell my staff—better is good, because you consolidate your gains and then you move on to the next fight from a stronger position....

So that's my advice. That's how you change things. Change isn't something that happens every four years or eight years; change is not placing your faith in any particular politician and then just putting your feet up and saying, okay, go. Change is the effort of committed citizens who hitch their wagons to something bigger than themselves and fight for it every single day.

Better is good, because you consolidate your gains and then you move on to the next fight from a stronger position.

...Each of us is only here because someone else faced down challenges for us. We are only who we are because someone else struggled and sacrificed for us.... That is the story of America. A story whispered by slaves in the cotton fields, the song of marchers in Selma, the dream of a King in the shadow of Lincoln. The prayer of immigrants who set out for a new world. The roar of women demanding the vote. The rallying cry of workers who built America. And the GIs who bled overseas for our freedom.

Now it's your turn. And the good news is, you're ready. And when your journey seems too hard, and when you run into a chorus of cynics who tell you that you're being foolish to keep believing or that you can't do something, or that you should just give up, or you should just settle—you might say to yourself a little phrase that I've found handy these last eight years: Yes, we can.

☆

We don't need perfect political systems; we need perfect participation.
–Cesar Chavez, United Farm Workers organizer and civil rights activist

Our democracy is dependent on each of us, and on our
active participation in the electoral process.
–Eric Holder, former U.S. attorney general

On the Results of the Election, November 9, 2016

PRESIDENT OBAMA: Good afternoon, everybody. Yesterday, before votes were tallied, I shot a video that some of you may have seen in which I said to the American people: Regardless of which side you were on in the election, regardless of whether your candidate won or lost, the sun would come up in the morning.

And that is one bit of prognosticating that actually came true. The sun is up. And I know everybody had a long night. I did, as well. I had a chance to talk to President-elect Trump last night—about 3:30 in the morning, I think it was—to congratulate him on winning the election. And I had a chance to invite him to come to the White House tomorrow to talk about making sure that there is a successful transition between our presidencies.

Now, it is no secret that the President-elect and I have some pretty significant differences. But remember, eight years ago, President Bush and I had some pretty significant differences. But President Bush's team could not have been more professional or more gracious in making sure we had a smooth transition so that we could hit the ground running. And one thing you realize quickly in this job is that the presidency, and the vice presidency, is bigger than any of us.

So I have instructed my team to follow the example that President Bush's team set eight years ago, and work as hard as we can to make sure that this is a successful transition for the President-elect—because we are now all rooting for his success in uniting and leading the country. The peaceful transition of power is one of the hallmarks of our democracy. And over the next few months, we are going to show that to the world....

Now, everybody is sad when their side loses an election. But the day after, we have to remember that we're actually all on one team.

Melanie Garunay, "President Obama Speaks on the Results of the Election: 'We Are Americans First,'" President Barack Obama White House archives, November 9, 2016, https://obamawhitehouse.archives.gov/blog/2016/11/09/president-obama-speaks-results-election.

This is an intramural scrimmage. We're not Democrats first. We're not Republicans first. We are Americans first. We're patriots first. We all want what's best for this country.... This was a long and hard-fought campaign. A lot of our fellow Americans are exultant today. A lot of Americans are less so. But that's the nature of campaigns. That's the nature of democracy. It is hard, and sometimes contentious and noisy, and it's not always inspiring.

But to the young people who got into politics for the first time, and may be disappointed by the results, I just want you to know, you have to stay encouraged. Don't get cynical. Don't ever think you can't make a difference.... Fighting for what is right is worth it.

Sometimes you lose an argument. Sometimes you lose an election....

The point, though, is, is that we all go forward, with a presumption of good faith in our fellow citizens—because that presumption of good faith is essential to a vibrant and functioning democracy. That's how this country has moved forward for 240 years. It's how we've pushed boundaries and promoted freedom around the world. That's how we've expanded the rights of our founding to reach all of our citizens. It's how we have come this far.

And that's why I'm confident that this incredible journey that we're on as Americans will go on. And I am looking forward to doing everything that I can to make sure that the next President is successful in that. I have said before, I think of this job as being a relay runner—you take the baton, you run your best race, and hopefully, by the time you hand it off you're a little further ahead, you've made a little progress. And I can say that we've done that, and I want to make sure that handoff is well-executed, because ultimately we're all on the same team.

☆

The likeliest reason why so many of us care so little about politics is that modern politicians make us sad, hurt us deep down in ways that are hard even to name, much less talk about. It's way easier to roll your eyes and not give a shit.

—David Foster Wallace, author

In the darkest times, hope is something you give yourself. That is the meaning of inner strength.

—Uncle Iroh, *Avatar: The Last Airbender*

The Hill We Climb—Amanda Gorman

Gorman read her poem at President Joseph Biden's inauguration, January 20, 2021.

When day comes, we ask ourselves where can we find light in this never-ending shade?
The loss we carry, a sea we must wade.
We've braved the belly of the beast.
We've learned that quiet isn't always peace,
and the norms and notions of what "just" is isn't always justice.
And yet, the dawn is ours before we knew it.
Somehow we do it.
Somehow we've weathered and witnessed a nation that isn't broken,
but simply unfinished.
We, the successors of a country and a time where a skinny Black girl descended from slaves and raised by a single mother can dream of becoming president, only to find herself reciting for one.

And yes, we are far from polished, far from pristine,
but that doesn't mean we are striving to form a union that is perfect.
We are striving to forge our union with purpose.
To compose a country committed to all cultures, colors, characters, and conditions of man.
And so we lift our gazes not to what stands between us, but what stands before us.
We close the divide because we know, to put our future first, we must first put our differences aside.
We lay down our arms so we can reach out our arms to one another.
We seek harm to none and harmony for all.
Let the globe, if nothing else, say this is true:
That even as we grieved, we grew.
That even as we hurt, we hoped.
That even as we tired, we tried.
That we'll forever be tied together, victorious.
Not because we will never again know defeat, but because we will never again sow division.

Scripture tells us to envision that everyone shall sit under their own vine and fig tree and no one shall make them afraid.
If we're to live up to our own time, then victory won't lie in the blade, but in all the bridges we've made.
That is the promise to glade, the hill we climb, if only we dare.
It's because being American is more than a pride we inherit.
It's the past we step into and how we repair it.
We've seen a force that would shatter our nation rather than share it.
Would destroy our country if it meant delaying democracy.
This effort very nearly succeeded.
But while democracy can be periodically delayed,
it can never be permanently defeated.
In this truth, in this faith, we trust,
for while we have our eyes on the future, history has its eyes on us.
This is the era of just redemption.
We feared it at its inception.
We did not feel prepared to be the heirs of such a terrifying hour,
but within it, we found the power to author a new chapter, to offer hope and laughter to ourselves.
So while once we asked, 'How could we possibly prevail over catastrophe?' now we assert, 'How could catastrophe possibly prevail over us?'

We will not march back to what was, but move to what shall be:
A country that is bruised but whole, benevolent but bold, fierce and free.
We will not be turned around or interrupted by intimidation because we know our inaction and inertia will be the inheritance of the next generation.
Our blunders become their burdens.
But one thing is certain:
If we merge mercy with might, and might with right, then love becomes our legacy and change, our children's birthright.

So let us leave behind a country better than the one we were left.
With every breath from my bronze-pounded chest, we will raise this wounded world into a wondrous one.
We will rise from the golden hills of the west.
We will rise from the wind-swept north-east where our forefathers first realized revolution.
We will rise from the lake-rimmed cities of the midwestern states.
We will rise from the sun-baked south.
We will rebuild, reconcile, and recover.
In every known nook of our nation, in every corner called our country,
our people, diverse and beautiful, will emerge, battered and beautiful.
When day comes, we step out of the shade, aflame and unafraid.
The new dawn blooms as we free it.
For there is always light,
if only we're brave enough to see it.
If only we're brave enough to be it.

CHAPTER 3

Black Americans and the Promise of Voting

My grandmother could not vote. My aunts and uncles could not vote at one time, and I made a promise to them that whenever I had the opportunity to have a say in our democracy, I would go to the polls in their honor and in my ancestors' honor.

—Janelle Monae, singer, songwriter

We are not helpless. The fire is still burning. Please go out and vote this November. So many people have died and sacrificed so much for us to have our voice, we have to use it. Get in formation. Use our voices to do something great for our children.

—Beyoncé, singer, songwriter, actor, entrepreneur

☆

The Safeguard of the Strongest; the Voice of the Weakest—Robert Purvis

Purvis was a free Black resident of Pennsylvania and a civil rights advocate.

In this 1838 speech, entitled "Appeal of Forty Thousand Citizens Threatened with Disenfranchisement, to the People of Pennsylvania," Purvis urged Pennsylvanians not to ratify a new state constitution that added the word "white" to the description of those permitted to vote. The vote had previously been extended to all "freemen," a term that was defined variously by different counties in the state.

Fellow Citizens: We appeal to you [in regard to] the decision of the "Reform Convention," which has stripped us of a right peaceably enjoyed during forty-seven years under the Constitution of this commonwealth. We honor Pennsylvania and her noble institutions too much to part with our birthright, as her free citizens, without a

---

"Appeal of Forty Thousand Citizens Threatened with Disenfranchisement, to the People of Pennsylvania," *The Colored American*, 1838, https://philadelphiaencyclopedia.org/essays/appeal-of-forty-thousand-citizens/.

struggle. To all her citizens the right of suffrage is valuable in proportion as she is free; but surely there are none who can so ill afford to spare it as ourselves.

It is the safeguard of the strongest that he lives under a government which is obliged to respect the voice of the weakest.

Was it the intention of the people of this commonwealth that the Convention to which the Constitution was committed for revision and amendment, should tear up and cast away its first principles? Was it made the business of the Convention to deny "that all men are born equally free," by making political rights depend upon the skin in which a man is born? or to divide what our fathers bled to unite, to wit, TAXATION and REPRESENTATION? We will not allow ourselves for one moment to suppose, that the majority of the people of Pennsylvania are not too respectful of the rights and too liberal towards the feelings of others, as well as too much enlightened to their own interests, to deprive of the right of suffrage a single individual who may safely be trusted with it. And we cannot believe that you have found among those who bear the burdens of taxation any who have proved, by their abuse of the right, that it is not safe in their hands. This is a question, fellow citizens, in which we plead your cause as well as our own.

It is the safeguard of the strongest that he lives under a government which is obliged to respect the voice of the weakest. When you have taken from an individual his right to vote, you have made the government, in regard to him, a mere despotism; and you have taken a step towards making it a despotism to all.... When a distinct class of the community, already sufficiently the objects of prejudice, are wholly, and for ever, disfranchised and excluded, to the remotest posterity, from the possibility of a voice in regard to the laws under which they are to live—it is the same thing as if their abode were transferred to the dominions of the Russian Autocrat, or of the Grand Turk. They have lost their check upon oppression, their wherewith to buy friends, their panoply of manhood; in short, they are thrown upon the mercy of a despotic majority. Like every other despot, this despot majority will believe in the mildness of its own sway, but who will the more willingly submit to it for that?

. . . We love our native country, much as it has wronged us; and in the peaceable exercise of our inalienable rights, we will cling to it. . . . We are Pennsylvanians, and we hope to see the day when Pennsylvania will have reason to be proud of us, as we believe she has now none to be ashamed. . . .

What have we done to forfeit the inestimable benefits of this charter? Why should tax-paying colored men, any more than other tax-payers, be deprived of the right of voting for their representatives? . . . We put it to the conscience of every Pennsylvanian, whether there is, or ever has been, in the commonwealth, either a political party or religious sect which has less deserved than ourselves to be thus disfranchised. . . . If we are bad citizens let them apply the proper remedies. . . . All we ask is, that no man shall be excluded on account of his color, that the same rule shall be applied to all.

☆

A man without a vote is a man without protection.
—Lyndon B. Johnson, former U.S. president

Your vote matters. Your voice matters. Your will matters. Your desire for yourself and your families matters, and regardless of who you are, where you live or what party you belong to, your vote matters. Your vote is your power, and I say don't ever let anyone take your power from you.
—Kamala Harris, U.S. vice president

A Severe Test—Abraham Lincoln

Lincoln was the U.S. president, 1861–1865.

Two days after Confederate General Robert E. Lee surrendered at Appomattox Court House on April 9, 1865, ending the Civil War, Lincoln voiced his support for Black suffrage for the first time publicly. John Wilkes Booth, an actor and a Confederate white supremacist, was in the crowd at the White House who were listening to Lincoln speak; enraged by Lincoln's support for Black voting, Booth promised, "That is the last speech he will make." Three days later, Booth shot Lincoln dead at Ford's Theater.

Quoted in Francis Bicknell Carpenter, *Six Months at the White House with Abraham Lincoln: The Story of a Picture*, August 1864

Carpenter, a painter, was given space for six months in the White House to make a painting commemorating the Emancipation Proclamation, which he completed in July 1864. His memoir of the time contains numerous anecdotes about Lincoln. In the following story, a friend, the secretary of a cabinet member, spoke with Lincoln about pessimism concerning the upcoming election.

My friend said that he found Mr. Lincoln alone, looking more than usually careworn and sad. Upon hearing the statement, he walked two or three times across the floor in silence. Returning, he said with grim earnestness of tone and manner: "Well, I cannot run the political machine; I have enough on my hands without that. It is the people's business,—the election is in their hands. If they turn their backs to the fire, and get scorched in the rear, they'll find they have got to 'sit' on the 'blister'!"

On the 1864 Election, in Response to a Serenade, November 10, 1864

Lincoln spoke on the question of holding a presidential election during the Civil War.

It has long been a grave question whether any government, not too strong for the liberties of its people, can be strong enough to maintain its own existence in great emergencies.

On this point the present rebellion brought our republic to a severe test; and a presidential election occurring in regular course during the rebellion added not a little to the strain. If the loyal people, united, were put to the utmost of their strength by the rebellion, must they not fail when divided, and partially paralized [*sic*], by a political war among themselves?

But the election was a necessity.

We can not have free government without elections; and if the rebellion could force us to forego, or postpone a national election, it might fairly claim to have already conquered and ruined us. The strife of the election is but human-nature practically applied to the facts of the case. What has occurred in this case, must ever recur in similar

Lincoln Home, National Historic Site, Illinois, "Lincoln on the 1864 Election," National Park Service, accessed March 15, 2024, https://www.nps.gov/liho/learn/historyculture/1864election.htm#.

cases. Human-nature will not change. In any future great national trial, compared with the men of this, we shall have as weak, and as strong; as silly and as wise; as bad and good. Let us, therefore, study the incidents of this, as philosophy to learn wisdom from, and none of them as wrongs to be revenged.

☆

The vote is a trust more delicate than any other, for it involves not just the interests of the voter but his life, honor, and future as well.
—Joseph Conrad, author

The everyday news of the world is often so overwhelming that it numbs us to other people's pain.... What can we do? How do we make a difference? Vote!
—Oprah Winfrey, television host, producer, actor, author

An Urgency to Obtain the Ballot—Frederick Douglass

Douglass was an abolitionist, reformer, speaker, and writer who escaped from slavery when he was twenty years old and who then became the most prominent leader of the movement for Black civil rights in the 1800s.

An Appeal to Congress for Impartial Suffrage, 1867

...Man is the only government-making animal in the world. His right to a participation in the production and operation of government is an inference from his nature, as direct and self-evident as is his right to acquire property or education. It is no less a crime against the manhood of a man, to declare that he shall not share in the making and directing of the government under which he lives, than to say that he shall not acquire property and education. The fundamental and unanswerable argument in favor of the enfranchisement of the negro is found in the undisputed fact of his manhood. He is a man, and by every fact and argument by which any man can sustain his right to vote, the negro can sustain his right equally. It is plain that, if the right belongs to any, it belongs to all. The doctrine that some men have no rights that others are bound to respect, is a doctrine which we must banish, as we

---

"An Appeal to Congress for Impartial Suffrage," *The Atlantic*, January 1867, https://www.theatlantic.com/magazine/archive/1867/01/an-appeal-to-congress-for-impartial-suffrage/306547/

have banished slavery, from which it emanated. If black men have no rights in the eyes of white men, of course the whites can have none in the eyes of the blacks. The result is a war of races, and the annihilation of all proper human relations.

Suffrage for the negro . . . is a measure of relief,—a shield to break the force of a blow already descending with violence, and render it harmless. . . .

Strong as we are, we need the energy that slumbers in the black man's arm to make us stronger. We want no longer any heavy-footed, melancholy service from the negro. We want the cheerful activity of the quickened manhood of these sable millions. Nor can we afford to endure the moral blight which the existence of a degraded and hated class must necessarily inflict upon any people among whom such a class may exist. . . .

If the right belongs to any,
it belongs to all.

. . . Disfranchisement in a republican government based upon the idea of human equality and universal suffrage, is a very different thing from disfranchisement in governments based upon the idea of the divine right of kings, or the entire subjugation of the masses. Masses of men can take care of themselves. . . . What is common to all works no special sense of degradation to any. But in a country like ours, where men of all nations, kindred, and tongues are freely enfranchised, and allowed to vote, to say to the negro, You shall not vote, is to deal his manhood a staggering blow, and to burn into his soul a bitter and goading sense of wrong, or else work in him a stupid indifference to all the elements of a manly character. . . . Casting aside all thought of justice and magnanimity, is it wise to impose upon the negro all the burdens involved in sustaining government against foes within and foes without, to make him equal sharer in all sacrifices for the public good, to tax him in peace and conscript him in war, and then coldly exclude him from the ballot-box?

Disguise it as we may, we are still a divided nation. . . . We have crushed the Rebellion, but not its hopes or its malign purposes. . . .

Statesmen of America! beware what you do. The ploughshare of rebellion has gone through the land beam-deep. The soil is in readiness, and the seedtime has come. Nations, not less than individuals, reap as they sow. The dreadful calamities of the past few years came not by accident, nor unbidden, from the ground. You shudder to-day at the harvest of blood sown in the spring-time of the Republic by your patriot fathers. The principle of slavery, which they tolerated under the erroneous impression that it would soon die out, became at last the dominant principle and power at the South. It early mastered the Constitution, became superior to the Union, and enthroned itself above the law. . . .

This evil principle again seeks admission into our body politic. It comes now in shape of a denial of political rights to four million loyal colored people. . . . Statesmen, beware what you do. The destiny of unborn and unnumbered generations is in your hands. Will you repeat the mistake of your fathers, who sinned ignorantly ? Or will you profit by the blood-bought wisdom all round you, and forever expel every vestige of the old abomination from our national borders? . . . Will the country be peaceful, united, and happy, or troubled, divided, and miserable?

☆

I believe in America's core promise—that you can come from humble circumstances and do great things. That has motivated generations of Americans to seek opportunity. Voting is the most important way to make our voices heard in pushing for change toward a better America in which all can prosper.

—Condoleezza Rice, former U.S. secretary of state

We Welcome the Fifteenth Amendment

At a meeting of the American Equal Rights Association, whose goal was to win suffrage for women, in New York, May 12–13, 1869, Douglass spoke in favor of proceeding with the ratification of the Fifteenth Amendment even though women still were denied the vote. Some suffragists, including Elizabeth Cady Stanton and Susan B. Anthony, insisted that Blacks should not win the right to vote before women did. Others there, such as Lucy Stone, supported the ratification of the amendment permitting Black and formerly enslaved citizens to vote while continuing the long struggle for women's voting rights.

"We Welcome the Fifteenth Amendment: Addresses Delivered in New York, New York, on May 12–13, 1869," Frederick Douglass Papers Project, accessed March 15, 2024, https://frederickdouglasspapersproject.com/s/digitaledition/item/18459.

MR. DOUGLASS—I must say that I do not see how any one can pretend that there is the same urgency in giving the ballot to women as to the negro. With us, the matter is a question of life and death. It is a matter of existence, at least, in fifteen states of the Union. When women, because they are women, are hunted down through the cities of New York and New Orleans; when they are dragged from their houses and hung upon lamp-posts; when their children are torn from their arms, and their brains dashed out upon the pavement; when they are objects of insult and outrage at every turn; when they are in danger of having their homes burnt down over their heads; when their children are not allowed to enter schools; then they will have an urgency to obtain the ballot equal to our own. (Great applause.)

Fifteenth Amendment, Section 1 (ratified February 3, 1870): The right of citizens of the United States to vote shall not be denied or abridged by the United States, or by any State, on account of race, color, or previous condition of servitude.

To America, 1917—James Weldon Johnson

Johnson was a writer and civil rights activist who was part of the leadership of the National Association for the Advancement of Colored People (NAACP).

How would you have us, as we are?
Or sinking 'neath the load we bear?
Our eyes fixed forward on a star?
Or gazing empty at despair?

Rising or falling? Men or things?
With dragging pace or footsteps fleet?
Strong, willing sinews in your wings?
Or tightening chains about your feet?

I believe voting is part of a deep responsibility I have to make this country better. Every right and liberty I enjoy has been voted into law. Now those of us who have those rights must vote in the interest of others. The world I want to live in isn't reflected in our government officials and that needs to change. That's why I'm voting.
—Megan Rapinoe, World Cup winner, Olympic medalist

Do not give in to the temptations of hopelessness, cynicism, or despair. That is exactly what opponents of democracy need to succeed.
—Alexandria Ocasio-Cortez, U.S. representative from New York

A Free Unfettered Right to Vote—James Clyburn

Clyburn has served in the House of Representatives as a Democrat from South Carolina since 1993.

In his remarks on the introduction of the John R. Lewis Voting Rights Advancement Act, September 19, 2023, Congressman Clyburn references a long history of suppression of Black voting rights in the South after Reconstruction ended in 1877. Practices including "literacy tests," poll taxes, intimidation, reprisals, and violence effectively denied Black people the right to vote for a hundred years following the ratification of the Fifteenth Amendment. The activists of the 1960s civil rights movement—many of them college students, as Clyburn and his eventual colleague in Congress, John Lewis, were—marched, organized, endured beatings and jail, and in some cases were even killed, in the cause of racial equality. Their efforts drew the attention of President Lyndon Johnson and Congress to the need for federal legislation aimed at enforcing the Fifteenth Amendment. The result was the Voting Rights Act of 1965 (discussed further in chapter 6).

Congressman Clyburn also references the *Slaughter-House Cases* of 1872, the first cases in the Supreme Court based on the two other post–Civil War amendments ratified along with the Fifteenth: the Thirteenth Amendment, abolishing slavery, and the Fourteenth, setting out the rights of the formerly enslaved. In the *Slaughter-House Cases*, the Supreme Court limited the reach of the Fourteenth Amendment so that it was ineffective in state and local matters. Congressman Clyburn compares that Supreme Court ruling with the 2013 Supreme Court decision *Shelby v. Holder*, which nullified Section 4 of the Voting Rights Act, weakening federal power to enforce voting rights.

"Congressman Clyburn Delivers Remarks on Intro of the John R. Lewis Voting Rights Advancement Act," video, September 18, 2023, YouTube, https://www.youtube.com/watch?v=n1SjVqFsPgQ.

Almost one hundred years after the Fifteenth Amendment became part of the Constitution, John Lewis and I first met as college students, 19-year-old college students, back in 1960, and several years ago, in the *Shelby v. Holder* case, when the Supreme Court handed down that decision, John and I talked a lot about the efforts that we had undertaken as college students and what that decision meant. We started talking about the throwback to those years when people in the South most especially were subjected to certain indignities, like counting or determining how many jelly beans were in a jar, in order to qualify to vote—or asked to interpret the Constitution, for people who could not even read the Constitution.

But then, in the run-up to the last presidential election, I started hearing things, started seeing things—they reminded me not so much of what we did out on the streets in the 1960s, but it reminded me of the things I was studying in the classrooms.

And one thing particularly came to mind, and I went back and I did the research to find it. I found it in this document, and it was a memorandum written by a man named Martin Witherspoon Gary, a confederate general from Edgefield, South Carolina, who wrote a memorandum... on how to go about nullifying the impact of... formerly enslaved African-Americans, who in the South were showing up in great numbers and holding office.

And they decided in the 1876 presidential election to nullify those votes.

And all that I was hearing during that campaign, and what I heard during that dreadful day that the insurrection took place in this building [on January 6, 2021], is all in this document.

This is nothing new. I'm convinced that those on the other side... studied it, and they did after the elections exactly what's in this document.

So this is not new.

And you see that ought to just unify the members of this Congress, to unify the people of this country.

Because unless we are looking forward to reliving those ten decades of Jim Crow that followed the *Slaughter-House Cases* of 1872, just like *Shelby v. Holder*, we are in for some tough times unless we can reauthorize this John R. Lewis Voting Rights Advancement Act, which will protect the franchise for people who are really believers in this democracy, people who have given their all to make sure that everybody has a free unfettered right to vote.

And you're not going to do that unless we can rally the American people to do things necessary to maintain this democracy and our greatness as a country.

☆

It's not enough to simply complain about injustice; the only way to prevent future injustice is to create the society we would like to see, one where we are all equal under the law.

—Al Sharpton, minister and civil rights activist

CHAPTER 4
Votes for Women

I know nothing of man's rights, or woman's rights;
human rights are all that I recognize.
—Sarah Moore Grimké, abolitionist and women's rights advocate

Wouldn't you want to be absolutely positive that the folks elected to make those decisions about our daily lives, decisions that range from when we send our troops to war to how victims of sexual assault are treated—wouldn't you want to be sure that those elected officials were thinking about all of us, not just some small percentage of us?
—Michelle Obama, former First Lady

☆

Is It a Crime to Vote?—Susan B. Anthony

Anthony was a women's rights activist and one of the most prominent leaders of the movement for equal rights for women in the 1800s. She gave this speech in 1872–73 after being arrested for unlawful voting.

Friends and Fellow-citizens: I stand before you to-night, under indictment for the alleged crime of having voted at the last Presidential election, without having a lawful right to vote. It shall be my work this evening to prove to you that in thus voting, I not only committed no crime, but, instead, simply exercised my citizen's right, guaranteed to me and all United States citizens by the National Constitution, beyond the power of any State to deny.

Our democratic-republican government is based on the idea of the natural right of every individual member thereof to a voice and a vote in making and executing the laws....

"All men are created equal, and endowed by their Creator with certain unalienable rights. Among these are life, liberty and the pursuit of happiness. That to secure these, governments are instituted among men, deriving their just powers from the consent of the governed."

"Address of Susan B. Anthony," speaking tour following 1872 arrest, *Famous Trials*, ed. Professor Douglas O. Linder, University of Missouri–Kansas City School of Law, accessed March 15, 2024, https://famous-trials.com/anthony/438-anthonyaddress.

Here is no shadow of government authority over rights, nor exclusion of any from their full and equal enjoyment. Here is pronounced the right of all men, and "consequently," as the Quaker preacher said, "of all women," to a voice in the government. And here, in this very first paragraph of the declaration, is the assertion of the natural right of all to the ballot; for, how can "the consent of the governed" be given, if the right to vote be denied....

...One-half of the people of this nation to-day are utterly powerless to blot from the statute books an unjust law, or to write there a new and a just one. The women, dissatisfied as they are with this form of government, that enforces taxation without representation, —that compels them to obey laws to which they have never given their consent, —that imprisons and hangs them without a trial by a jury of their peers, —that robs them, in marriage, of the custody of their own persons, wages and children, —are this half of the people left wholly at the mercy of the other half, in direct violation of the spirit and letter of the declarations of the framers of this government, every one of which was based on the immutable principle of equal rights to all....

How can "the consent of the governed" be given, if the right to vote be denied?

The preamble of the federal constitution says:

"We, the people of the United States, in order to form a more perfect union, establish justice, insure domestic tranquility, provide for the common defense, promote the general welfare and secure the blessings of liberty to ourselves and our posterity, do ordain and established this constitution for the United States of America."

It was we, the people, not we, the white male citizens, nor yet we, the male citizens; but we, the whole people, who formed this Union. And we formed it, not to give the blessings of liberty, but to secure them; not to the half of ourselves and the half of our posterity, but to the whole people—women as well as men. And it is downright mockery to talk to women of their enjoyment of the blessings of liberty while they are denied the use of the only means of securing them provided by this democratic-republican government—the ballot....

...We all know that American citizenship, without addition or qualification, means the possession of equal rights, civil and political.

We all know that the crowning glory of every citizen of the United States is, that he can either give or withhold his vote from every law and every legislator under the government....

And it is upon this just interpretation of the United States Constitution that our National Woman Suffrage Association which celebrates the twenty-fifth anniversary of the woman's rights movement in New York on the 6th of May next, has based all its arguments and action the past five years.

We no longer petition Legislature or Congress to give us the right to vote. We appeal to the women everywhere to exercise their too long neglected "citizen's right to vote." We appeal to the inspectors of election everywhere to receive the votes of all United States citizens as it is their duty to do....

We ask the juries to fail to return verdicts of "guilty" against honest, law-abiding, tax-paying United States citizens for offering their votes at our elections....

We ask the judges to render true and unprejudiced opinions of the law, and wherever there is room for a doubt to give its benefit on the side of liberty and equal rights to women, remembering that "the true rule of interpretation under our national constitution, especially since its amendments, is that anything for human rights is constitutional, everything against human rights unconstitutional."

And it is on this line that we propose to fight our battle for the ballot—all peaceably, but nevertheless persistently through to complete triumph, when all United States citizens shall be recognized as equals before the law.

☆

The young women of today, free to study, to speak, to write, to choose their occupation, should remember that every inch of this freedom was bought for them at a great price.
—Abigail Scott Duniway, writer, editor, and lecturer

If change is what you want, nothing will change unless you take action. So please, if you are old enough, please get out there and speak up. P.S. I'm so grateful to have been able to vote because it wasn't too long ago women didn't even have those rights... see what happens when we demand change?
—Demi Lovato, singer, actor

A Great Truth—Frederick Douglass

Douglass was an abolitionist, reformer, speaker, and writer. In his speech before the International Council of Women in April 1888, Douglass recalled his presence at the first women's rights convention in the United States, in Seneca Falls, New York, in 1848. He had disagreed about ratification of the Fifteenth Amendment with suffragists such as Elizabeth Cady Stanton and Susan B. Anthony, who did not believe that Black men should have the right to vote before women did, but he continued to be a strong supporter of votes for women in the years that followed.

...When I look around on this assembly, and see the many able and eloquent women, full of the subject, ready to speak, and who only need the opportunity to impress this audience with their views and thrill them with "thoughts that breathe and words that burn," I do not feel like taking up more than a very small space of your time and attention, and shall not. I would not, even now, presume to speak, but for the circumstance of my early connection with the cause, and of having been called upon to do so by one whose voice in this Council we all gladly obey. Men have very little business here as speakers, anyhow; and if they come here at all they should take back benches and wrap themselves in silence. For this is an International Council, not of men, but of women, and woman should have all the say in it. This is her day in court.

I do not mean to exalt the intellect of woman above man's; but I have heard many men speak on this subject, some of them the most eloquent to be found anywhere in the country; and I believe no man, however gifted with thought and speech, can voice the wrongs and present the demands of women with the skill and effect, with the power and authority of woman herself.... Woman knows and feels her wrongs as man cannot know and feel them, and she also knows as well as he can know, what measures are needed to redress them.... She is her own best representative. We can neither speak for her, nor vote for her, nor act for her, nor be responsible for her; and the thing for men to do in the premises is just to get out of her way and give her the fullest opportunity to exercise all the powers inherent in her individual personality, and allow her to do it as she herself shall elect to exercise them. Her right to be and to do is as full, complete, and perfect as the right of any man on earth. I say of her, as I say of the colored people, "Give her fair play, and hands off."

"Frederick Douglass on Woman Suffrage (1888)," *BlackPast*, January 28, 2007, https://www.blackpast.org/african-american-history/speeches-african-american-history/1888-frederick-douglass-woman-suffrage/.

There was a time when, perhaps, we men could help a little. It was when this woman suffrage cause was in its cradle, when it was not big enough to go alone, when it had to be taken in the arms of its mother from Seneca Falls, N.Y., to Rochester, N.Y., for baptism. I then went along with it and offered my services to help it, for then it needed help; but now it can afford to dispense with me and all of my sex. Then its friends were few—now its friends are many. Then it was wrapped in obscurity—now it is lifted in sight of the whole civilized world, and people of all lands and languages give it their hearty support. Truly the change is vast and wonderful....

When a great truth once gets abroad in the world, no power on earth can imprison it, or prescribe its limits, or suppress it.

At this distance of time from that convention at Rochester, and in view of the present position of the question, it is hard to realize the moral courage it required to launch this unwelcome movement. Any man can be brave when the danger is over, go to the front when there is no resistance, rejoice when the battle is fought and the victory is won; but it is not so easy to venture upon a field untried with one-half the whole world against you, as these women did....

There are few facts in my humble history to which I look back with more satisfaction than to the fact, recorded in the history of the woman-suffrage movement, that I was sufficiently enlightened at that early day, and when only a few years from slavery, to support your resolution for woman suffrage. I have done very little in this world in which to glory except this one act—and I certainly glory in that. When I ran away from slavery, it was for myself; when I advocated emancipation, it was for my people; but when I stood up for the rights of woman, self was out of the question, and I found a little nobility in the act....

All good causes are mutually helpful. The benefits accruing from this movement for the equal rights of woman are not confined or limited to woman only. They will be shared by every effort to promote the progress and welfare of mankind everywhere and in all ages. It was an example and a prophecy of what can be accomplished against strongly opposing forces, against time-hallowed abuses, against deeply entrenched error, against worldwide usage, and against the settled judgment of mankind, by a few earnest women, clad only in the panoply of truth, and determined to live and die in what they considered a righteous cause.

...Whatever the future may have in store for us, one thing is certain—this new revolution in human thought will never go backward. When a great truth once gets abroad in the world, no power on earth can imprison it, or prescribe its limits, or suppress it. It is bound to go on till it becomes the thought of the world. Such a truth is woman's right to equal liberty with man. She was born with it. It was hers before she comprehended it. It is inscribed upon all the powers and faculties of her soul, and no custom, law or usage can ever destroy it. Now that it has got fairly fixed in the minds of the few, it is bound to become fixed in the minds of the many, and be supported at last by a great cloud of witnesses, which no man can number and no power can withstand....

☆

Summoning all my strength, I shouted at the top of my voice: "How about votes for women?" You would have thought I had thrown a bomb.
—Alice Paul, suffragist and author of the original Equal Rights Amendment

Human rights are women's rights—and women's rights are human rights. Let us not forget that among those rights are the right to speak freely, and the right to be heard.
—Hillary Rodham Clinton, former First Lady, U.S. senator, and candidate for president

A Happier Nation—Carrie Chapman Catt

Catt was president of the National American Woman Suffrage Association when the Nineteenth Amendment was ratified. She went on to found the League of Women Voters.

Address to the Congress on Women's Suffrage, November 1917, Washington, DC

"Address to the Congress on Women's Suffrage, Delivered November 1917," *American Rhetoric: Top 100 Speeches*, accessed March 15, 2024, https://www.americanrhetoric.com/speeches/carriechapmancattsuffragespeech.htm.

Woman suffrage is inevitable.... Three distinct causes made it inevitable.

First, the history of our country. Ours is a nation born of revolution, of rebellion against a system of government so securely entrenched in the customs and traditions of human society that in 1776 it seemed impregnable. From the beginning of things, nations had been ruled by kings and for kings, while the people served and paid the cost. The American Revolutionists boldly proclaimed the heresies: "Taxation without representation is tyranny." "Governments derive their just powers from the consent of the governed." The colonists won, and the nation which was established as a result of their victory has held unfailingly that these two fundamental principles of democratic government are not only the spiritual source of our national existence but have been our chief historic pride and at all times the sheet anchor of our liberties.

Eighty years after the Revolution, Abraham Lincoln welded those two maxims into a new one: "Ours is a government of the people, by the people, and for the people." Fifty years more passed and the president of the United States, Woodrow Wilson, in a mighty crisis of the nation, proclaimed to the world: "We are fighting for the things which we have always carried nearest to our hearts: for democracy, for the right of those who submit to authority to have a voice in their own government."...

"There is one thing mightier than kings and armies...the power of an idea when its time has come."

With such a history behind it, how can our nation escape the logic it has never failed to follow, when its last un-enfranchised class calls for the vote? Behold our Uncle Sam floating the banner with one hand, "Taxation without representation is tyranny," and with the other seizing the billions of dollars paid in taxes by women to whom he refuses "representation." Behold him again, welcoming the boys of twenty-one and the newly made immigrant citizen to "a voice in their own government" while he denies that fundamental right of democracy to thousands of women public school teachers from whom many of these men learn all they know of citizenship and patriotism, to women college presidents, to women who preach in our pulpits, interpret law in our courts, preside over our hospitals, write books and magazines, and serve in every uplifting moral and social enterprise. Is there a single man who can justify such inequality of treatment, such outrageous discrimination? Not one....

Second, the suffrage for women already established in the United States makes women suffrage for the nation inevitable.... Our nation cannot long continue a condition under which government in half its territory rests upon the consent of half of the people and in the other half upon the consent of all the people; a condition which grants representation to the taxed in half of its territory and denies it in the other half; a condition which permits women in some states to share in the election of the president, senators, and representatives and denies them that privilege in others....

Third, the leadership of the United States in world democracy compels the enfranchisement of its own women. The maxims of the Declaration were once called "fundamental principles of government." They are now called "American principles" or even "Americanisms." They have become the slogans of every movement toward political liberty the world around, of every effort to widen the suffrage for men or women in any land. Not a people, race, or class striving for freedom is there anywhere in the world that has not made our axioms the chief weapon of the struggle....

Your party platforms have pledged women suffrage. Then...why not put the amendment through Congress and the legislatures? We shall all be better friends, we shall have a happier nation, we women will be free to support loyally the party of our choice, and we shall be far prouder of our history.

"There is one thing mightier than kings and armies"—aye, than Congresses and political parties—"the power of an idea when its time has come to move." The time for woman suffrage has come. The woman's hour has struck. If parties prefer to postpone action longer and thus do battle with this idea, they challenge the inevitable. The idea will not perish; the party which opposes it may....

☆

The right to be seen, the right to be heard, the right to direct the course of history are markers of power.

—Stacey Abrams, lawyer and former Georgia state representative

Voting is the only way to ensure that your concerns matter. Period.
—Michelle Obama, former First Lady

Why Woman Wants to Vote—Helen Keller

Keller lost her sight as a baby but went on to become a well-known author, activist, and lecturer. This essay was published in 1920.

We demand the vote, not because we think we are better or wiser than men, but because it is our right as much as it is theirs. And even if we all vote together, we cannot abuse this right more than the men have done by themselves. There is already a good deal wrong with the world—anyone who reads at all intelligently knows that. Perhaps one of the chief reasons for the chaotic conditions of things is that the world has been trying to get along with only half of itself. The two parts are unlike, and it takes both to make a whole.

We demand the vote for women because it is in accordance with the principles of a true democracy. Many labor under the delusion that we live in a democracy. I have to smile—several ways—when I read that ours is "a government of the people, by the people, and for the people." We are neither a democracy nor a true representative republic. We are a government of parties and partisans, and lo, at least half the adult population may not even belong to these parties! We demand woman suffrage also because without it women cannot protect themselves and their children. Some people like to imagine that the chivalrous nature of man will constrain him to act humanely towards woman and protect her rights. SOME men do protect some women. We demand that all women have the right to protect themselves.

Political power, intelligently used, enables the citizen to direct and shape the legal affairs of the state and determine what shall be the relations of human beings to each other, individually and collectively. Without this power, women who do not happen to have a "natural protector" are at the mercy of man-made laws, and experience shows that these laws are often unjust to them. In some states of this "enlightened democracy" of men, the father is the sole owner of the child. I believe he can even will away the unborn babe. In some states women cannot hold property, and their wages belong to their

"Speech Given by Helen Keller in Favor of Women's Suffrage Entitled 'Why Woman Wants to Vote,' 1920," Helen Keller Archive, American Foundation for the Blind, accessed March 15, 2024, https://www.afb.org/HelenKellerArchive?a=d&d=A-HK02-B212-F05-002&.

fathers or their husbands. Legislation concerning the age of consent is another proof that the voice of woman is mute in the halls of the law-makers. Surely, women are not isolated beings, puppets in the world to be manipulated by men.

Rights are things which we get when we are strong enough to make our claim to them good.

Anyway, the fight is on, and I advise any man who is still hesitating to hurry up and get on the right side. For there will soon be a terrific struggle between democracy and autocracy—as a matter of fact, it has begun.

Their old-fashioned ideas are up a tree, and traditions are breaking up, and the new plans are arriving. It is time to take a good look.

We do not want a woman's world or a man's, but a human world no longer cursed by misery, ignorance, disease and crime. We want a world where there is fair play in every relation of life—an equitable distribution of human comfort and happiness, a just amount of labor for everyone, a real living wage, the security of every worker from oppression of one or many. Everywhere, in all countries, in all classes we see woman-force running to waste that should be utilized in making the world a decent home for all humanity.

There are no such things as "divine, immutable, inalienable rights." Rights are things which we get when we are strong enough to make our claim to them good. Today women are asserting their rights; tomorrow nobody will be foolhardy enough to question them.

Nineteenth Amendment (ratified by the states August 18, 1920): The right of citizens of the United States to vote shall not be denied or abridged by the United States or by any State on account of sex. Congress shall have power to enforce this article by appropriate legislation.

How to Interest Women in Voting—Eleanor Roosevelt

Roosevelt, spouse of President Franklin Roosevelt, was the First Lady from 1933 to 1945, as well as an activist and diplomat. This essay was published in 1924.

The most difficult problem before women leaders today is "How are we to interest the women of the state in voting and get them to change from their uninterested and apathetic attitude to an attitude of intelligent and active interest in their Government?" I sometimes think that women have used their vote a little as a small child uses his first garden. He plants his seeds with great care, but instead of watering them and giving them constant care and attention, he forgets all about them, or else digs them up to see what they are doing. We have treated our vote the same way. We dig it up now and then, but we give it very little care in between times. Of course, no one woman has the right to say what the mass of women want to accomplish with their vote, but I can at least say what I hope the Democratic women wish to achieve.

First: Honest, clean administration in party organizations, coupled with a real desire to have the people understand fundamental issues. The trouble is the means for knowing the truth are very few, and I consider that it is one of the real duties of political parties to state clearly and plainly their belief and the things for which they stand.

We cannot expect that our wishes will be respected unless we learn to use the tools which give us strength.

Second: We want to see a real use of the primaries so that they will express the will of the people. The real primary used by all the people is a great opportunity for expressing the will of the many. We women are not as yet on a completely equal basis in the party organizations, therefore, we, above all, should realize the opportunity afforded to us in the primaries, where we can see that the candidates we wish are placed on the ballot by petition, or if that is impossible, we can organize and write in any name that we desire. We cannot expect that our wishes will

"How to Interest Women in Voting: An Entry by Mrs. Eleanor Roosevelt in the Women's Democratic Campaign Manual, 1924," Social Welfare History Project, Virginia Commonwealth University Libraries, accessed March 15, 2024, https://socialwelfare.library.vcu.edu/woman-suffrage/how-to-interest-women-in-voting/.

be respected unless we learn to use the tools which give us strength, and unless we are willing to work for the things we believe in.

Third: We desire to see a greater interest taken by our Government in what is best for the mass of the people, as opposed to groups among the people. This does not mean that I am unmindful of the necessity that business must prosper and that capital should have its just reward, but the balance must be kept proportionate among the various activities of our people; those who manufacture, those who till the soil, those who work for science, art, and education all alike must prosper for the better development of the human race and the country.

Fourth: From this interest in the mass of our own people, we wish to see a growth in the real interest taken in the welfare of the world as a whole. Without this real interest we will not enter any League or Association of nations, we will take no steps to prevent war, we will remain selfish individuals, each scrambling for our own little place in the sun... forgetting that the great cloud over others may easily spread and cover our little patch of sun as well.

☆

If American women would increase their voting turnout by ten percent, I think we would see an end to all of the budget cuts in programs benefiting women and children.

—Coretta Scott King, author, civil rights leader, and widow of Martin Luther King, Jr.

If we don't have representation and we don't have women's voices helping to shape the debate, then we leave a vacuum. It's important not just for women to run, but for women who do run to be committed to the women's rights agenda, to the democracy agenda, to be on the side of making it easier to vote, to ensuring that the votes are counted correctly.

—Hillary Rodham Clinton, former First Lady, U.S. senator, and candidate for president

Phone Call—Laura Bush and Effie Hobby

Bush, spouse of President George W. Bush, was First Lady from 2001 to 2009. On November 4, 2002, she called Ms. Effie Hobby, a Connecticut resident who had voted in every election since women gained voting rights in 1920, to thank her for voting.

MRS. BUSH: Effie, are you there?

MS. HOBBY: Yes, I'm here.

MRS. BUSH: Good. This is Laura Bush. And I'm so excited to call you and thank you for voting every year, every election since you started voting, since women first got the right to vote.

MS. HOBBY: Who am I talking to?

MRS. BUSH: You're talking to Laura Bush.

MS. HOBBY: My goodness. Happy birthday.

MRS. BUSH: Oh, why, thank you very much. Thanks for that. I'm so excited to get to talk to you, after you've had so many birthdays.

MS. HOBBY: I surely have. (Laughter.)

MRS. BUSH: Can you remember what it was like when you first voted, when women first got to vote in the United States?

MS. HOBBY: Surely.

MRS. BUSH: Surely. Did most women show up at the polls?

MS. HOBBY: No.

MRS. BUSH: No.

MS. HOBBY: It's so exciting, though.

MRS. BUSH: I'm sure it was really exciting. I got to stand on the steps of the Texas Governor's Mansion on the 75th anniversary of women suffrage, with my mother and my daughters. And that was really fun, to think about how women first started to vote in the United States, and to get to be there with my mother, who was a little girl when that happened, and my daughters, who I hope will carry on the family tradition of voting at every election.

Why do you think it's so important for women to vote?

MS. HOBBY: Sorry?

MRS. BUSH: Why do you think it's important.

MS. HOBBY: Why I do?

MRS. BUSH: Yes, for women to vote.

"Remarks by Mrs. Laura Bush in Telephone Conversation with Ms. Effie Hobby, Connecticut Resident Who Has Voted in Every Election Since 1920, When Women Gained Voting Rights," President George W. Bush White House Archives, November 8, 2002, https://georgewbush-whitehouse.archives.gov/news/releases/2002/11/20021108.html.

MS. HOBBY: I think they should—I think maybe they're going a little too far, but I think it's a good idea. (Laughter.)

MRS. BUSH: Absolutely, because they have that right. What's the secret to your long life?

MS. HOBBY: Heritage.

MRS. BUSH: Heritage. That's probably also the secret to your long history of voting, too, is it?

MS. HOBBY: Yes.

MRS. BUSH: Did your parents always vote?

MS. HOBBY: Republican.

MRS. BUSH: They always voted Republican?

MS. HOBBY: I vote Republican always, nationally.

MRS. BUSH: Well, I appreciate that.

MS. HOBBY: After that, I think whoever I think is—

MRS. BUSH: Yes, the best man for the local races?

MS. HOBBY: That's it.

MRS. BUSH: And I understand you voted for our good friend, John Rowland, too, for governor.

MS. HOBBY: There was no question—(Laughter.)

MRS. BUSH: That's great. Well, Effie, thank you. It's such a pleasure for me to get to talk to you.

MS. HOBBY: It's amazing for me to talk to you. I never expected this, for sure. (Laughter.)

MRS. BUSH: Well, you're a very, very good model for all the rest of us, for all women in America, that you've been voting since the very first time, the very first year of women's suffrage, and that you've always voted.

MS. HOBBY: Give your husband my regards, and tell him I wish I always agreed with him.

MRS. BUSH: Okay, I sure will. Thank you so much, Effie, and congratulations on so many years of voting.

MS. HOBBY: Thank you very much.

MRS. BUSH: Bye. Lots of love.

MS. HOBBY: Thank you.

MRS. BUSH: Bye-bye.

Life is a hard battle anyway. If we laugh and sing a little as we fight the good fight of freedom, it makes it all go easier.
—Sojourner Truth, abolitionist and women's rights advocate

Searching for Equality—Ruth Bader Ginsburg

Ginsburg was a justice of the U.S. Supreme Court from 1993 to 2020.

The Nineteenth Amendment and Beyond; A Conversation Between United States Supreme Court Justice Ruth Bader Ginsburg and Ninth Circuit Court of Appeals Judge M. Margaret McKeown, February 10, 2020

JUDGE MCKEOWN:... We're here tonight to celebrate the 100th anniversary of the Nineteenth Amendment. While your career has focused on equality very broadly, I want to go back in time and talk about the Amendment. You said at one point that you wished your mother could have lived in an age when women could aspire and achieve, and when daughters were treated equally to sons.

JUSTICE GINSBURG: When daughters were cherished as much as sons.

JUDGE MCKEOWN: So, what do you imagine your mother would have been or done had she lived in such an age? And is it true that she marched on behalf of the Nineteenth Amendment?

JUSTICE GINSBURG: Yes, my mother was eighteen when the Nineteenth Amendment became part of the Constitution. When she was fifteen and sixteen, she marched in parades in New York. My mother's mind was bright as could be. She might have been a university professor, or a university president, or a legal luminary, but those occupations were far beyond her reach. She grew up in a large family. Six of her siblings survived into adulthood. She graduated high school at age fifteen. Only one child in her family was a university graduate, the eldest son. My mother went to work at age fifteen to help support the family, which would gain no income from the eldest son during his years at Cornell University. If any child would have a university education, it would not be the eldest or any daughter. It would be the eldest son.

"Searching for Equality: The Nineteenth Amendment and Beyond; A Conversation Between United States Supreme Court Justice Ruth Bader Ginsburg and Ninth Circuit Court of Appeals Judge M. Margaret McKeown," *Georgetown Law Journal* 108, no. 5 (2020), https://www.law.georgetown.edu/georgetown-law-journal/wp-content/uploads/sites/26/2020/07/Searching-for-Equality-The-Nineteenth-Amendment-and-Beyond.pdf.

JUDGE MCKEOWN: . . . In your view, what is the legacy of the Nineteenth Amendment?

JUSTICE GINSBURG: It was the first step toward equal-citizenship stature for women. Some of the suffragists had high hopes for the Nineteenth Amendment. Strictly, it says the right to vote shall not be denied or abridged on account of sex. But if women were to have equality in the political domain—that is, if they were part of the political constituency and could vote—then how could you abide subordination of women in the civil domain? For example, if a woman wanted a loan, she had to get her husband's permission or he had to sign for it. The courts interpreted the Nineteenth Amendment strictly, said it gave the women the right to vote and nothing more. One of the controversies concerned women serving on juries. In the not-so-good-old days, women weren't called for jury duty. Another was running for office. Yet passage of the Nineteenth Amendment was a miracle of sorts because everyone who voted for it, in Congress and in the states, was male. The suffragists had to sell votes for women to an all-male audience, and that was no easy task. But many of them hoped it would do more than allow women to vote.

I mentioned jury duty and running for office. The National Woman's Party was the more radical wing of the Suffrage Movement. In its members' view, if the Nineteenth Amendment was going to be interpreted restrictively, we needed something else. So they introduced the Equal Rights Amendment in 1923, and almost every year thereafter, until at last Congress let it out. The Nineteenth Amendment was the beginning, but strong feminists believed women should have equality in all fields of human endeavor, so we needed an Equal Rights Amendment [ERA]. In my view, we still do. . . .

JUDGE MCKEOWN: . . . There's a great story about the Nineteenth Amendment. Tennessee was the last to give the right to women; and there was a particular legislator who was inclined to vote against it. But his mother that morning put a little note in his pocket, and basically said, "Do the right thing."

JUSTICE GINSBURG: "Be a good boy."

JUDGE MCKEOWN: "Be a good boy." So, I think it pays to listen to your mother, because he ultimately voted in favor of the Amendment. And then, of course, that vote pushed the Amendment over the line and we got the Nineteenth Amendment. . . .

JUDGE MCKEOWN: . . . So, here's a related question . . . although women formally won the vote 100 years ago, many young women of color are still disenfranchised, particularly through restrictive voting laws. What is your comment on that in terms of where we are going in the voting-rights arena?

Passage of the Nineteenth Amendment was a miracle of sorts because everyone who voted for it, in Congress and in the states, was male.

JUSTICE GINSBURG: I'm pleased that one of my former law clerks is spending a good deal of her time getting eighteen-year-olds to register to vote, especially minority women. She goes with them to the registration place. I think that young people are going to make a difference. What our government does now will affect their lives, so they should care deeply about exercising the right to vote. And there should be concerted efforts to see that before they go to vote, they are registered properly.

☆

It's about more than just politics... it's about the character of our country. It's about decency and doing what is right for all people.... TRUTH over lies. UNITY over division. SCIENCE over fiction. HOPE over fear. The world is waiting for YOU!!!!! Your leadership. Get out and vote like you've never voted before!! Your voice matters.

—Jennifer Lopez, dancer, singer, actor

A lot of women suffered and sacrificed for decades to give me this right. I will always vote because democracy is a precious luxury.

—Meghan McCain, television personality and author

CHAPTER 5
Old Enough to Fight, Old Enough to Vote

More young people voted in 2020 than in any election since the 26th Amendment was ratified in 1971, lowering the voting age from 21 to 18. And several hot-button issues like climate change and abortion are important to this demographic.
—Dan Rather, journalist and news anchor

If I vote and you don't, my vote counts double. And it's not just the fringes who benefit—the fact is that it is to some very powerful Establishments' advantage that most younger people hate politics and don't vote.
—David Foster Wallace, author

☆

This Fateful Summons—Dwight D. Eisenhower

Eisenhower was a five-star general during World War II and the U.S. president, 1953–1961.

State of the Union Address: Suffrage, 1954

My few remaining recommendations all relate to a basic right of our citizens—that of being represented in the decisions of the government.

I hope that the States will cooperate with the Congress in adopting uniform standards in their voting laws that will make it possible for our citizens in the armed forces overseas to vote. In the District of Columbia the time is long overdue for granting national suffrage to its citizens and also applying the principle of local self-government to the Nation's Capital. I urge the Congress to move promptly in this direction....

For years our citizens between the ages of 18 and 21 have, in time of peril, been summoned to fight for America. They should participate

---

"Eisenhower's State of the Union Address, 1954," *American Experience*, PBS, accessed March 15, 2024, https://www.pbs.org/wgbh/americanexperience/features/eisenhower-state54/.

in the political process that produces this fateful summons. I urge Congress to propose to the States a constitutional amendment permitting citizens to vote when they reach the age of 18.

☆

One of the penalties for refusing to participate in politics
is that you end up being governed by your inferiors.
—Plato, ancient philosopher

I wanted to remind you guys to vote the people
who most represent YOU into power.
—Taylor Swift, singer, songwriter

A New Arena—Edward M. Kennedy

Kennedy served as a U.S. senator from Massachusetts from 1962 to 2009.

Lowering the National Voting Age to 18: Testimony Before the Senate Subcommittee on Constitutional Amendments, March 9, 1970

. . . I believe the time has come to lower the voting age in the United States, and thereby to bring American youth into the mainstream of our political process. To me, this is the most important single principle we can pursue as a nation if we are to succeed in bringing our youth into full and lasting participation in our institutions of democratic government. . . .

First, our young people today are far better equipped—intellectually, physically, and emotionally—to make the type of choices involved in voting than were past generations of youth. . . . Because of the enormous impact of modern communications, especially television, our youth are extremely well informed on all the crucial issues of our time, foreign and domestic, national and local, urban and rural. . . .

Second, by lowering the voting age to 18, we will encourage civic responsibility at an earlier age, and thereby promote lasting social involvement and political participation for our youth. . . .

"Lowering the National Voting Age to 18: Testimony Before the Senate Subcommittee on Constitutional Amendments, March 9, 1970," *In His Own Words*, Senator Edward M. Kennedy, http://www.tedkennedy.org/ownwords/event/voting_age/.

We will enlarge the meaning of participatory democracy in our society. We will give our youth a new arena for their idealism, activism, and energy.... Third, 18-year-olds already have many rights and responsibilities in our society comparable to voting. It does not automatically follow of course—simply because an 18-year-old goes to war, or works, or marries, or makes a contract, or pays taxes, or drives a car, or owns a gun, or is held criminally responsible, like an adult—that he should thereby be entitled to vote. Each right or responsibility in our society presents unique questions dependent on the particular issue at stake....

The well-known proposition—"old enough to fight, old enough to vote"—deserves special mention.... At the very least, the opportunity to vote should be granted in recognition of the risks an 18-year-old is obliged to assume when he is sent off to fight and perhaps die for his country. About 30% of our forces in Vietnam are under 21. Over 19,000, or almost half, of those who have died in action there were under 21. Can we really maintain that these young men did not deserve the right to vote?

Long ago, according to historians, the age of maturity was fixed at 21 because that was the age at which a young man was thought to be capable of bearing armor. Strange as it may seem, the weight of armor in the 11th century governs the right to vote of Americans in the 20th century. The medieval justification has an especially bitter relevance today, when millions of our 18-year-olds are compelled to bear arms as soldiers, and thousands are dead in Vietnam.... A society that imposes the extraordinary burden of war and death on its youth should also grant the benefit of full citizenship and representation, especially in sensitive and basic areas like the right to vote....

About 30% of our forces in Vietnam are under 21. Over 19,000, or almost half, of those who have died in action there were under 21.

...By lowering the voting age we will improve the overall quality of our electorate, and make it more truly representative of our society. By adding our youth to the electorate, we will gain a group of enthusiastic, sensitive, idealistic and vigorous new voters....

The right to vote is the fundamental political right in our Constitutional system. It is the cornerstone of all our other basic rights. It guarantees that our democracy will be government of the people and by the people, not just for the people. By securing the right to vote, we help to insure, in the historic words of the Massachusetts Bill of Rights, that our government "may be a government of laws, and not of men." Millions of young Americans have earned the right to vote, and we in Congress should respond....

Twenty-Sixth Amendment, Section 1 (ratified July 1, 1971): The right of citizens of the United States, who are eighteen years of age or older, shall not be denied or abridged by the United States or by any State on account of age.

Building the Future—Joseph Biden

Biden, who served as President Barack Obama's vice president, was sworn in as the U.S. president on January 20, 2021.

A Proclamation on the 50th Anniversary of the 26th Amendment, June 30, 2021

Our Constitution recognizes that, as a Nation, we are constantly learning. Our Founders built that recognition into its original design, providing a mechanism to amend our Constitution as our Nation evolved. On July 1, 1971, our Nation ratified the 26th Amendment to the Constitution, lowering the voting age to 18. At the time, 18-, 19-, and 20-year-old Americans were fulfilling their civic duties: paying taxes, serving in our Armed Forces, acting as first responders, laboring in fields, factories, and service jobs across the country, and pursuing higher education. They were participating in our democracy and all of the responsibilities of citizenship in all ways except for one: they could not vote. A broad coalition, following in the footsteps of the suffragettes of the early 20th century and the civil rights activists of the 1960s, advocated, educated, and prevailed in persuading our Nation that those younger Americans were entitled to the right to vote. We also made a

"A Proclamation on the 50th Anniversary of the 26th Amendment," White House, June 30, 2021, https://www.whitehouse.gov/briefing-room/presidential-actions/2021/06/30/a-proclamation-on-the-50th-anniversary-of-the-26th-amendment/.

national commitment that the right to vote would never be denied or abridged for any adult voter based on their age.

My first race for the Senate was one of the first elections in which 18-year-olds could vote, and the energy and passion of Delaware's young people helped propel me to an unlikely victory.

Fifty years later, younger voters remain essential to our civic infrastructure. They are not only voting in our elections—including at record rates in 2020—but winning them. Younger Americans are lending their talent and vision to school boards, city councils, and county commissions; teenagers are serving as State legislators and mayors, and we are the better for it.

Younger voters are not waiting to inherit the future; they are building the future themselves. Young Americans have been on the front lines in the fight to defend the right to vote and expand access to the ballot box for all eligible voters. Their civic engagement extends beyond voting—with young Americans leading the calls for racial justice, climate action, gun violence prevention, and immigration reform among many other issues.

Despite the progress we have made, there remain persistent gaps in turnout between younger voters and their older counterparts. There is still more that we can and must do to deliver on the promise of the 26th Amendment....

Today, we honor the bipartisan expansion of voter enfranchisement. Let us continue our work to make the 26th Constitutional Amendment ever more meaningful in the months and years ahead.

☆

The candidates and measures being voted on...have the power to impact millions of lives—and impact issues like access to abortion care, how we respond to climate change, the rights of trans youth, and more.... If all of us vote and encourage all of our loved ones to vote with us, we will truly be able to create a change.

—Ariana Grande, singer, songwriter, actor

CHAPTER 6
Voter Suppression and Voting Rights Enforcement

All kinds of genuine obstacles...have been intentionally placed to keep people from participating in democracy and mattering in democracy.... But what we have to remind ourselves, and each other, is that our democracy only works for us if we show up.
—America Ferrera, actor, director, producer

The right to vote, free from discrimination based on race or language, requires our vigilant protection. We know from many decades of long, hard struggle that the best way to defend a right is to go out and exercise it.
—Eric Holder, former U.S. attorney general

☆

Give Us the Ballot—Martin Luther King, Jr.

At the Prayer Pilgrimage for Freedom, a rally held May 17, 1957 (the third anniversary of the Supreme Court decision *Brown v. Board of Education*, which invalidated racial segregation), on the steps of the Lincoln Memorial in Washington, D.C., Dr. Martin Luther King, Jr.—a minister, civil rights leader, and political philosopher who was assassinated in 1968—called on the president and Congress to ensure long-denied voting rights for Black Americans.

Mr. Chairman, distinguished platform associates, fellow Americans. Three years ago the Supreme Court of this nation rendered in simple, eloquent, and unequivocal language a decision which will long be stenciled on the mental sheets of succeeding generations. For all men of goodwill, this May seventeenth decision came as a joyous daybreak to end the long night of human captivity. It came as a great beacon light of hope to millions of disinherited people throughout the world who had dared only to dream of freedom.

Unfortunately, this noble and sublime decision has not gone without opposition. This opposition has often risen to ominous proportions.

"Give Us the Ballot," May 17, 1957, https://kinginstitute.stanford.edu/king-papers/documents/give-us-ballot-address-delivered-prayer-pilgrimage-freedom.

Many states have risen up in open defiance. The legislative halls of the South ring loud with such words as "interposition" and "nullification."

But even more, all types of conniving methods are still being used to prevent Negroes from becoming registered voters. The denial of this sacred right is a tragic betrayal of the highest mandates of our democratic tradition. And so our most urgent request to the president of the United States and every member of Congress is to give us the right to vote. [Audience:] (Yes)

Give us the ballot, and we will no longer have to worry the federal government about our basic rights.

Give us the ballot (Yes), and we will no longer plead to the federal government for passage of an anti-lynching law; we will by the power of our vote write the law on the statute books of the South (All right) and bring an end to the dastardly acts of the hooded perpetrators of violence.

Give us the ballot (Give us the ballot), and we will transform the salient misdeeds of bloodthirsty mobs (Yeah) into the calculated good deeds of orderly citizens.

Give us the ballot (Give us the ballot), and we will fill our legislative halls with men of goodwill (All right now) and send to the sacred halls of Congress men who will not sign a "Southern Manifesto" because of their devotion to the manifesto of justice. (Tell 'em about it)

Give us the ballot (Yeah), and we will place judges on the benches of the South who will do justly and love mercy (Yeah), and we will place at the head of the southern states governors who will, who have felt not only the tang of the human, but the glow of the Divine.

Give us the ballot (Yes), and we will quietly and nonviolently, without rancor or bitterness, implement the Supreme Court's decision of May seventeenth, 1954. (That's right)

In this juncture of our nation's history, there is an urgent need for dedicated and courageous leadership. If we are to solve the problems ahead and make racial justice a reality, this leadership must be fourfold.

First, there is need for strong, aggressive leadership from the federal government. So far, only the judicial branch of the government has evinced this quality of leadership. If the executive and legislative branches of the government were as concerned about the protection of our citizenship rights as the federal courts have been, then the transition from a segregated to an integrated society would be infinitely smoother. But we so often look to Washington in vain for this concern.

In the midst of the tragic breakdown of law and order, the executive branch of the government is all too silent and apathetic. In the midst of the desperate need for civil rights legislation, the legislative branch of the government is all too stagnant and hypocritical.

This dearth of positive leadership from the federal government is not confined to one particular political party. Both political parties have betrayed the cause of justice. (Oh yes) The Democrats have betrayed it by capitulating to the prejudices and undemocratic practices of the southern Dixiecrats. The Republicans have betrayed it by capitulating to the blatant hypocrisy of right wing, reactionary northerners. These men so often have a high blood pressure of words and an anemia of deeds. [laughter]

The hour is late. The clock of destiny is ticking. We must act now, before it is too late.

In the midst of these prevailing conditions, we come to Washington today pleading with the president and members of Congress to provide a strong, moral, and courageous leadership for a situation that cannot permanently be evaded. We come humbly to say to the men in the forefront of our government that the civil rights issue is not an ephemeral, evanescent domestic issue that can be kicked about by reactionary guardians of the status quo; it is rather an eternal moral issue which may well determine the destiny of our nation (Yeah) in the ideological struggle with communism. The hour is late. The clock of destiny is ticking out. We must act now, before it is too late.

A second area in which there is need for strong leadership is from the white northern liberals. There is a dire need today for a liberalism which is truly liberal. What we are witnessing today in so many northern communities is a sort of quasi-liberalism which is based on the principle of looking sympathetically at all sides. It is a liberalism so bent on seeing all sides, that it fails to become committed to either side. It is a liberalism that is so objectively analytical that it is not subjectively committed. It is a liberalism which is neither hot nor cold, but lukewarm. (All right) We call for a liberalism from the North which will be thoroughly committed to the ideal of racial justice and will not be deterred by the propaganda and subtle words of those who say: "Slow up for a while; you're pushing too fast."

A third source that we must look to for strong leadership is from the moderates of the white South. It is unfortunate that at this time the leadership of the white South stems from the close-minded reactionaries. These persons gain prominence and power by the dissemination of false ideas and by deliberately appealing to the deepest hate responses within the human mind. It is my firm belief that this close-minded, reactionary, recalcitrant group constitutes a numerical minority. There are in the white South more open-minded moderates than appears on the surface. These persons are silent today because of fear of social, political and economic reprisals. God grant that the white moderates of the South will rise up courageously, without fear, and take up the leadership in this tense period of transition.

I cannot close without stressing the urgent need for strong, courageous and intelligent leadership from the Negro community. We need a leadership that is calm and yet positive. This is no day for the rabble-rouser, whether he be Negro or white. (All right) We must realize that we are grappling with the most weighty social problem of this nation, and in grappling with such a complex problem there is no place for misguided emotionalism. (All right, That's right) We must work passionately and unrelentingly for the goal of freedom, but we must be sure that our hands are clean in the struggle. We must never struggle with falsehood, hate, or malice. We must never become bitter. I know how we feel sometime. There is the danger that those of us who have been forced so long to stand amid the tragic midnight of oppression—those of us who have been trampled over, those of us who have been kicked about—there is the danger that we will become bitter. But if we will become bitter and indulge in hate campaigns, the new order which is emerging will be nothing but a duplication of the old order. (Yeah, That's all right)

We must meet hate with love. (Yeah) We must meet physical force with soul force. There is still a voice crying out through the vista of time, saying: "Love your enemies (Yeah), bless them that curse you (Yes), pray for them that despitefully use you." (That's right, All right) Then, and only then, can you matriculate into the university of eternal life. That same voice cries out in terms lifted to cosmic proportions: "He who lives by the sword will perish by the sword." (Yeah, Lord) And history is replete with the bleached bones of nations (Yeah) that failed to follow this command. (All right) We must follow nonviolence and love. (Yes, Lord)

Now, I'm not talking about a sentimental, shallow kind of love. (Go ahead) I'm not talking about eros, which is a sort of aesthetic, romantic love. I'm not even talking about philia, which is a sort of intimate affection between personal friends. But I'm talking about agape. (Yes sir) I'm talking about the love of God in the hearts of men. (Yes) I'm talking about a type of love which will cause you to love the person who does the evil deed while hating the deed that the person does. (Go ahead) We've got to love. (Oh yes)

There is another warning signal. We talk a great deal about our rights, and rightly so. We proudly proclaim that three-fourths of the peoples of the world are colored. We have the privilege of noticing in our generation the great drama of freedom and independence as it unfolds in Asia and Africa. All of these things are in line with the unfolding work of Providence. But we must be sure that we accept them in the right spirit. We must not seek to use our emerging freedom and our growing power to do the same thing to the white minority that has been done to us for so many centuries. (Yes) Our aim must never be to defeat or humiliate the white man. We must not become victimized with a philosophy of black supremacy. God is not interested merely in freeing black men and brown men and yellow men, but God is interested in freeing the whole human race. (Yes, All right) We must work with determination to create a society (Yes), not where black men are superior and other men are inferior and vice versa, but a society in which all men will live together as brothers (Yes) and respect the dignity and worth of human personality. (Yes)

We must also avoid the temptation of being victimized with a psychology of victors. We have won marvelous victories. Through the work of the NAACP, we have been able to do some of the most amazing things of this generation. And I come this afternoon with nothing, nothing but praise for this great organization, the work that it has already done and the work that it will do in the future. And although they're outlawed in Alabama and other states, the fact still remains that this organization has done more to achieve civil rights for Negroes than any other organization we can point to. (Yeah, Amen) Certainly, this is fine.

But we must not, however, remain satisfied with a court victory over our white brothers. We must respond to every decision with an understanding of those who have opposed us and with an appreciation of the difficult adjustments that the court orders pose for them. We must act in such a way as to make possible a coming together of white people and colored people on the basis of a real harmony of interest and understanding. We must seek an integration based on mutual respect.

I conclude by saying that each of us must keep faith in the future. Let us not despair. Let us realize that as we struggle for justice and freedom, we have cosmic companionship. This is the long faith of the Hebraic-Christian tradition: that God is not some Aristotelian "unmoved mover" who merely contemplates upon Himself. He is not merely a self-knowing God, but an other-loving God (Yeah) forever working through history for the establishment of His kingdom.

Keep going today. Keep moving amid every obstacle. Keep moving amid every mountain of opposition.

And those of us who call the name of Jesus Christ find something of an event in our Christian faith that tells us this. There is something in our faith that says to us, "Never despair; never give up; never feel that the cause of righteousness and justice is doomed." There is something in our Christian faith, at the center of it, which says to us that Good Friday may occupy the throne for a day, but ultimately it must give way to the triumphant beat of the drums of Easter. (That's right) There is something in our faith that says evil may so shape events that Caesar will occupy the palace and Christ the cross (That's right), but one day that same Christ will rise up and split history into A.D. and B.C. (Yes), so that even the name, the life of Caesar must be dated by his name. (Yes) There is something in this universe (Yes, Yes) which justifies Carlyle in saying: "No lie can live forever." (All right) There is something in this universe which justifies William Cullen Bryant in saying: "Truth crushed to earth will rise again." (Yes, All right) There is something in this universe (Watch yourself) which justifies James Russell Lowell in saying:

Truth forever on the scaffold,
Wrong forever on the throne. (Oh yeah)
Yet that scaffold sways the future,

And behind the dim unknown
Stands God (All right), within the shadow,
Keeping watch above His own. (Yeah, Yes)

Go out with that faith today. (All right, Yes) Go back to your homes in the Southland to that faith, with that faith today. Go back to Philadelphia, to New York, to Detroit and Chicago with that faith today (That's right), that the universe is on our side in the struggle. (Sure is, Yes) Stand up for justice. (Yes) Sometimes it gets hard, but it is always difficult to get out of Egypt, for the Red Sea always stands before you with discouraging dimensions. (Yes) And even after you've crossed the Red Sea, you have to move through a wilderness with prodigious hilltops of evil (Yes) and gigantic mountains of opposition. (Yes) But I say to you this afternoon: Keep moving. (Go on ahead) Let nothing slow you up. (Go on ahead) Move on with dignity and honor and respectability. (Yes)

I realize that it will cause restless nights sometime. It might cause losing a job; it will cause suffering and sacrifice. (That's right) It might even cause physical death for some. But if physical death is the price that some must pay (Yes sir) to free their children from a permanent life of psychological death (Yes sir), then nothing can be more Christian. (Yes sir) Keep going today. (Yes sir) Keep moving amid every obstacle. (Yes sir) Keep moving amid every mountain of opposition. (Yes sir, Yeah) If you will do that with dignity (Say it), when the history books are written in the future, the historians will have to look back and say, "There lived a great people. (Yes sir, Yes) A people with 'fleecy locks and black complexion,' but a people who injected new meaning into the veins of civilization (Yes); a people which stood up with dignity and honor and saved Western civilization in her darkest hour (Yes); a people that gave new integrity and a new dimension of love to our civilization." (Yeah, Look out) When that happens, "the morning stars will sing together (Yes sir), and the sons of God will shout for joy." (Yes sir, All right) [applause] (Yes, That's wonderful, All right)

☆

Voter suppression works its might by first tripping and causing to stumble the unwanted voter, then by convincing those who see the obstacle course to forfeit the race without even starting to run.

—Stacey Abrams, lawyer and former Georgia state representative

The Time for Waiting Is Gone—Lyndon B. Johnson

Johnson was the U.S. president, 1963–1969.

He began pushing the Voting Rights Act of 1965 through Congress days after peaceful civil rights marchers were attacked, beaten, and killed on "Bloody Sunday" in Selma, Alabama.

Address on Voting Rights to Joint Session of Congress, March 15, 1965

...At times, history and fate meet at a single time in a single place to shape a turning point in man's unending search for freedom.

So it was at Lexington and Concord. So it was a century ago at Appomattox. So it was last week in Selma, Alabama.

There, long suffering men and women peacefully protested the denial of their rights as Americans. Many were brutally assaulted. One good man—a man of God—was killed.

There is no cause for pride in what has happened in Selma. There is no cause for self-satisfaction in the long denial of equal rights of millions of Americans. But there is cause for hope and for faith in our democracy in what is happening here tonight.

For the cries of pain and the hymns and protests of oppressed people have summoned into convocation all the majesty of this great Government—the Government of the greatest nation on earth.

Our mission is at once the oldest and the most basic of this country—to right wrong, to do justice, to serve man.

In our time we have come to live with the moments of great crisis. Our lives have been marked with debate about great issues, issues of war and peace, issues of prosperity and depression.

But rarely in any time does an issue lay bare the secret heart of America itself. Rarely are we met with a challenge, not to our growth or abundance, or our welfare or our security, but rather to the values and the purposes and the meaning of our beloved nation.

The issue of equal rights for American Negroes is such an issue.

And should we defeat every enemy, and should we double our wealth and conquer the stars, and still be unequal to this issue, then we will have failed as a people and as a nation.

"Transcript of the Johnson Address on Voting Rights to Joint Session of Congress," *New York Times*, March 16, 1965, https://archive.nytimes.com/www.nytimes.com/books/98/04/12/specials/johnson-rightsadd.html.

For, with a country as with a person, "What is man profited if he shall gain the whole world, and lose his own soul?"

There is no Negro problem. There is no Southern problem. There is no Northern problem. There is only an American problem.

And we are met here tonight as Americans—not as Democrats or Republicans; we're met here as Americans to solve that problem.

This was the first nation in the history of the world to be founded with a purpose. The great phrases of that purpose still sound in every American heart, North and South:

"All men are created equal." "Government by consent of the governed." "Give me liberty or give me death."

And those are not just clever words, and those are not just empty theories.

Should we defeat every enemy, and should we double our wealth and conquer the stars, and still be unequal to this issue, then we will have failed as a people and as a nation.

In their name Americans have fought and died for two centuries and tonight around the world they stand there as guardians of our liberty risking their lives.

Those words are promised to every citizen that he shall share in the dignity of man. This dignity cannot be found in a man's possessions. It cannot be found in his power or in his position. It really rests on his right to be treated as a man equal in opportunity to all others.

It says that he shall share in freedom. He shall choose his leaders, educate his children, provide for his family according to his ability and his merits as a human being.

To apply any other test, to deny a man his hopes because of his color or race or his religion or the place of his birth is not only to do injustice. It is to deny America and to dishonor the dead who gave their lives for American freedom. . . .

> The vote is the most powerful instrument ever devised by man for breaking down injustice and destroying the terrible walls which imprison men because they are different from other men.
> —Lyndon B. Johnson, former U.S. president

Remarks in the Capitol Rotunda at the Signing of the Voting Rights Act, August 6, 1965

...Today is a triumph for freedom as huge as any victory that has ever been won on any battlefield. Yet to seize the meaning of this day, we must recall darker times.

Three and a half centuries ago the first Negroes arrived at Jamestown. They did not arrive in brave ships in search of a home for freedom. They did not mingle fear and joy, in expectation that in this New World anything would be possible to a man strong enough to reach for it.

They came in darkness and they came in chains.

And today we strike away the last major shackle of those fierce and ancient bonds. Today the Negro story and the American story fuse and blend.

And let us remember that it was not always so. The stories of our Nation and of the American Negro are like two great rivers. Welling up from that tiny Jamestown spring they flow through the centuries along divided channels.

When pioneers subdued a continent to the need of man, they did not tame it for the Negro. When the Liberty Bell rang out in Philadelphia, it did not toll for the Negro. When Andrew Jackson threw open the doors of democracy, they did not open for the Negro.

It was only at Appomattox, a century ago, that an American victory was also a Negro victory. And the two rivers—one shining with promise, the other dark-stained with oppression—began to move toward one another.

Yet, for almost a century the promise of that day was not fulfilled. Today is a towering and certain mark that, in this generation, that promise will be kept. In our time the two currents will finally mingle and rush as one great stream across the uncertain and the marvelous years of the America that is yet to come.

"Remarks in the Capitol Rotunda at the Signing of the Voting Rights Act, August 6, 1965," *American Presidency Project*, University of California, Santa Barbara, https://www.presidency.ucsb.edu/documents/remarks-the-capitol-rotunda-the-signing-the-voting-rights-act.

This act flows from a clear and simple wrong. Its only purpose is to right that wrong. Millions of Americans are denied the right to vote because of their color. This law will ensure them the right to vote. The wrong is one which no American, in his heart, can justify. The right is one which no American, true to our principles, can deny. . . .

The Members of the Congress, and the many private citizens, who worked to shape and pass this bill will share a place of honor in our history for this one act alone.

There were those who said this is an old injustice, and there is no need to hurry. But 95 years have passed since the 15th amendment gave all Negroes the right to vote.

Through this act, and its enforcement, an important instrument of freedom passes into the hands of millions . . . who have been denied the right to vote.

And the time for waiting is gone.

There were those who said smaller and more gradual measures should be tried. But they had been tried. For years and years they had been tried, and tried, and tried, and they had failed, and failed, and failed.

And the time for failure is gone.

There were those who said that this is a many-sided and very complex problem. But however viewed, the denial of the right to vote is still a deadly wrong.

And the time for injustice has gone.

This law covers many pages. But the heart of the act is plain. Wherever, by clear and objective standards, States and counties are using regulations, or laws, or tests to deny the right to vote, then they will be struck down. If it is clear that State officials still intend to discriminate, then Federal examiners will be sent in to register all eligible voters. When the prospect of discrimination is gone, the examiners will be immediately withdrawn.

And, under this act, if any county anywhere in this Nation does not want Federal intervention it need only open its polling places to all of its people.

...Through this act, and its enforcement, an important instrument of freedom passes into the hands of millions of our citizens. But that instrument must be used. Presidents and Congresses, laws and lawsuits can open the doors to the polling places and open the doors to the wondrous rewards which await the wise use of the ballot.

But only the individual Negro, and all others who have been denied the right to vote, can really walk through those doors, and can use that right, and can transform the vote into an instrument of justice and fulfillment....

☆

It isn't about who is the majority in Congress. It's about, are people educated and enfranchised and resourced enough to participate in the government that purports to be of the people, by the people, for the people? We're missing the people part—and not because people don't care, but because we're not doing our job as a country, as a culture, to make democracy work.

—America Ferrera, actor, director, producer

Here's the problem: while some folks are frustrated and tuned out and staying home on election day, trust me, other folks are showing up. Democracy continues with or without you.

—Michelle Obama, former First Lady

Every Citizen Is a Somebody—George W. Bush

Bush was the U.S. president, 2001–2009.

Remarks on Signing Voting Rights Act Reauthorization and Amendments Act of 2006, July 27, 2006

...America began with a Declaration that all men are created equal. This Declaration marked a tremendous advance in the story of freedom, yet it also contained a contradiction: Some of the same men who signed their names to this self-evident truth owned other men as property. By reauthorizing this act, Congress has reaffirmed its belief

"President Bush Signs Voting Rights Act Reauthorization and Amendments Act of 2006," Office of the Press Secretary, White House, July 27, 2006, https://georgewbush-whitehouse.archives.gov/news/releases/2006/07/20060727.html.

that all men are created equal; its belief that the new founding started by the signing of the bill by President Johnson is worthy of our great nation to continue. (Applause.)...

The right of ordinary men and women to determine their own political future lies at the heart of the American experiment, and it is a right that has been won by the sacrifice of patriots. The Declaration of Independence was born on the stand for liberty taken at Lexington and Concord. The amendments to our Constitution that outlawed slavery and guaranteed the right to vote came at the price of a terrible civil war.

The Voting Rights Act that broke the segregationist lock on the ballot box rose from the courage shown on a Selma bridge one Sunday afternoon in March of 1965. On that day, African Americans, including a member of the United States Congress, John Lewis—(applause)—marched across the Edmund Pettus Bridge in a protest intended to highlight the unfair practices that kept them off the voter rolls.

In the America promised by our founders, every citizen is a somebody.

The brutal response showed America why a march was necessary. When the marchers reached the far side of the bridge, they were met by state troopers and a civilian posse bearing billy clubs and whips—weapons they did not hesitate to use. The images of policemen using nightsticks on peaceful protestors were carried on television screens across the country, and they stung the conscience of a slumbering America.

One week after Selma, President Lyndon Johnson took to the airwaves to announce that he planned to submit legislation that would bring African Americans into the civic life of our nation. Five months after Selma, he signed the Voting Rights Act into law in the Rotunda of our nation's Capitol. (Applause.) In a little more than a year after Selma, a newly enfranchised black community used their power at the ballot box to help defeat the sheriff who had sent men with whips and clubs to the Edmund Pettus Bridge on that bloody Sunday.

For some parts of our country, the Voting Rights Act marked the first appearance of African Americans on the voting rolls since Reconstruction. And in the primaries and elections that followed the signing of this act, many African Americans pulled the voting lever for the first time in their lives.

Eighty-one year old Willie Bolden was the grandson of slaves, and in the spring of 1966, he cast his first ballot in Alabama's Democratic primary. He told a reporter, "It felt good to me. It made me think I was sort of somebody." In the America promised by our founders, every citizen is a somebody, and every generation has a responsibility to add its own chapter to the unfolding story of freedom. (Applause.)

In four decades since the Voting Rights Act was first passed, we've made progress toward equality, yet the work for a more perfect union is never ending. We'll continue to build on the legal equality won by the civil rights movement to help ensure that every person enjoys the opportunity that this great land of liberty offers. And that means a decent education and a good school for every child, a chance to own their own home or business, and the hope that comes from knowing that you can rise in our society by hard work and God-given talents. (Applause.)...

☆

Democracy is the only system that persists in asking the powers that be whether they are the powers that ought to be.

—Sydney J. Harris, newspaper columnist

It's not the voting that's democracy; it's the counting.

—Tom Stoppard, playwright

Keep Pushing—Barack Obama

Obama was the U.S. president, 2009–2017.

Remarks by the President on the Voting Rights Act, August 6, 2015

...As John [Lewis] indicated, 50 years ago today, President Johnson signed the Voting Rights Act into law to protect this precious right. It broke down legal barriers at the state level and at the local level that were keeping African Americans from exercising their constitutional right to vote. And all of us have a great debt to not just John Lewis, but the thousands—many of them unnamed—who were courageous enough

"Remarks by the President on the Voting Rights Act," Office of the Press Secretary, White House, August 6, 2015, https://obamawhitehouse.archives.gov/the-press-office/2015/08/06/remarks-president-voting-rights-act.

to walk up and try to register time and time again, that were threatened because of their efforts to register—sharecroppers and maids and ordinary folks. Had it not been for them awakening the conscience of a nation, the President could not have mustered the political support that was required to ultimately get this seminal law passed.

We had the opportunity to honor some of the sacrifices that were made earlier this year in Selma, along with 100 members of Congress—Democratic and Republican members. It was heartening to see the bipartisan attendance. It signified that in the abstract, at least, everybody today believes in the right to vote. Conceptually, everybody is in favor of the right to vote. (Laughter and applause.) You will not hear anybody defend the notion that the law can discriminate against persons because of their color, or their faith, or their ethnicity, when it comes to going to cast a ballot. That's huge progress, a normative shift in how we think about our democracy. Everybody in theory is supposed to be included.

But part of the reason we're here today, part of the reason it's so important for us to focus attention on this right is because in practice, we've still got problems.

On the ground, there are still too many ways in which people are discouraged from voting. Some of the protections that had been enshrined in the Voting Rights Act itself have been weakened as a consequence of court decisions and interpretations of the law. State legislatures have instituted procedures and practices that, although on the surface may appear neutral, have the effect of discouraging people from voting, may have a disproportional effect on certain kinds of folks voting.

And if, in fact, those practices, those trends, those tendencies are allowed to continue unanswered, then over time the hard-won battles of 50 years ago erode, and our democracy erodes. And that means that the decisions that are made in the corridors of power all across this country begin to reflect the interests of the few, instead of the interests of the many.

So we've got serious business to attend to here. One order of business is for our Congress to pass an updated version of the Voting Rights Act that would correct some of the problems that have arisen. (Applause.)

... There's legislation pending. There are people of goodwill on both sides of the aisle who are prepared to move it. But it keeps on slipping as a priority. Part of the reason we're here is to reaffirm to members of Congress, this has to be a priority. (Applause.) If this isn't working then nothing is working. We've got to get it done. (Applause.)

> Far more people disenfranchise themselves than any law does by not participating, by not getting involved.

At the state levels, we've got some outstanding members of state legislatures—California, Florida—who have been championing mechanisms to get more people voting: Early voting, online registration. But sadly, too many states are making it harder for folks to vote—instituting photo ID laws that on the surface sound good; if you poll the average American, they'll say, yes, you have to show your photo ID. But in practice, it turns out that for seniors and for poorer folks, that's not always easy to do. And by the way, it doesn't actually address a real problem because there are almost no instances of people going to vote in somebody else's name. (Applause.) It's just not a—it turns out it's just not a common crime. (Laughter.)

Folks might think about shoplifting. Attorney General, you know more about the crime statistics than I do, but I am certain, because we've actually looked at the data on this, that almost nobody wakes up saying, I'm going to go vote in somebody else's name. (Laughter.) Doesn't happen. So the only reason to pass this law, despite the reasonableness of how it sounds, is to make it harder for folks to vote.

You've got state legislatures that are rolling back early voting. I don't understand why anybody would be opposed to spreading out voting so that people can arrange to vote depending on their schedule. Because it's hard—if you are working the midnight shift, and got to get your kid to school, and had to travel by bus, and you're a single mom—it may be difficult for you to be able to vote precisely in that window that's provided. And there's no evidence that, as a consequence of early voting, that has increased fraud; that people somehow have become less committed to democracy; they don't feel that same sense of civic pride as they do if there's just one day of voting. There's no evidence of that. The reason to roll back early voting is because you want to make it harder for folks to vote.

So, in theory everybody is in favor of the right to vote. In practice, we have state legislatures that are deliberately trying to make it harder for people to vote.

And some of them, frankly, are not that shy about saying so. (Laughter.) Think about that. Think about that. How can you rationalize making it harder for people to vote? How can you rationalize penalizing people because they don't have a lot of money not being able to vote? That's contrary to who we are. That's not what we believe. That's not what John Lewis fought for. In the United States of America, we should have no patience and no tolerance for laws that aim at disenfranchising our fellow citizens.

So we got to keep pushing. At the federal level, we need a new Voting Rights Act passed. At the state and local levels, we've got to fight back against efforts to make it harder to vote and we got to embrace those legislators that are prepared to make it easier to vote.

But there's one last aspect to this, and that is the job of citizens in actually exercising the franchise. This isn't always a popular thing to say in front of progressive groups—everybody is fired up, and rightly so. But the reason that the voting rate in the last midterm election was 30-something percent is not attributable to a photo I.D. law. The fact of the matter is that far more people disenfranchise themselves than any law does by not participating, by not getting involved.

Seize the power that you have.
Make this democracy work.

So, yes, we have to be vigilant in pushing back against laws that seek to disenfranchise people. Yes, we should be fighting back against laws, for example, that say ex-felons, no matter how long they've been living a correct life, no matter how well they've paid their dues, that they can never vote again in that state. There are all kinds of battles we have to fight. But we miss the forest for the trees if we don't also recognize that huge chunks of us, citizens, just give away our power. We'd rather complain than do something about it. We won't vote, and then we'll talk about the terrible political process that isn't doing anything.

And I like barber shop talk. (Laughter.) I like grumbling and complaining. I can't always do it in public. (Laughter.) But what I know is it doesn't get anything accomplished. So the groups that are here today, one of the things that we're looking forward to is how do we mobilize, how do we galvanize, how do we get people focused not only on laws but also on our habits—our habits of citizenship? How do we instill in people a sense of why this is so critically important?

...The bottom line is everybody here has a part to play. Members of Congress need to do the right thing. State legislators and governors, they need to do the right thing. Businesses—make it easier for your employees to vote. Do the right thing. Universities, other civic institutions—help register people to vote; provide civic education. Do the right thing.

Most of all, citizens—seize the power that you have. Make this democracy work. Do not succumb to cynicism. Heroic things happen when people get involved. Heroic things happen when a young man without any official title joins up with a bunch of other young and not-so-young people of every color and every persuasion and are willing to march across a bridge. That's the power that is in all of us. We've got to take advantage of it.

☆

Voting allows us to make America more free, more just, and more equal for all. We can't wait for someone else to act. We have to be out there, fighting for our country and making its promises a reality. Because on our worst day, we are blessed to live in America.

—Nikki Haley, former U.S. ambassador to the United Nations

Voting is the expression of our commitment to ourselves, one another, this country, and this world.

—Sharon Salzberg, author and mindfulness teacher

We Need to Fix It and Fix It Now—John Lewis

Lewis was a Democratic representative from Georgia from 1987 to 2020.

Speech on House Floor in Support of the Voter Empowerment Act, July 18, 2018

In a democracy, the right to vote is the most powerful nonviolent tool we have.

"Rep. John Lewis on the Right to Vote," YouTube, July 18, 2018, https://www.youtube.com/watch?v=h5i_qelqm5U.

Many people marched and protested for the right to vote.

Some gave a little blood.

And others lost their lives.

Some of you have heard me say that the right to vote is precious, almost sacred.

In my heart of hearts, I believe that we should make it simple and convenient for all of our citizens to be part of the democratic process.

It should not matter whether you're Black or White, Latino, Asian American or Native American.

We should be able to participate in the democratic process.

On March 7, 1965, I gave a little blood on the Edmund Pettus Bridge for the right to vote.

Before the Voting Rights Act of 1965 was passed, some people had to count the number of jelly beans in a jar, and all across America today, when people go out to attempt to vote, they stand in long, immoveable lines.

That's not right.

It's not fair.

And it's not just.

We can do better and we must do better.

We have a moral obligation, a mission, and a mandate to empower all of the American people, not just a select few.

We must do what is right, what is fair, and what is just.

Today our democracy is under attack by forces within and forces abroad.

We need to fix it and fix it now....

☆

It is time for a resurrection and not an insurrection.... We won't be silent anymore. If we have to make Election Day a labor strike day, we will.

—William Barber II, minister and social activist

Bring a friend or two...bring your neighbor, a member of your family, and together, cast a vote for your country and be willing to do whatever it takes to stand up for what you believe in.

—Lady Gaga, singer, actor

Your Vote Is Your Voice, and Your Voice Is Your Human Dignity—Raphael Warnock

Warnock is a U.S. senator, representing Georgia since 2021.

First Senate Floor Speech, March 17, 2021

. . . At the time of my birth, Georgia's two senators were Richard B. Russell and Herman E. Talmadge, both arch segregationists and unabashed adversaries of the civil rights movement. After the Supreme Court's landmark *Brown v. Board* ruling outlawing school segregation, Talmadge warned that "blood will run in the streets of Atlanta." Senator Talmadge's father, Eugene Talmadge, former governor of our state, had famously declared, "The South loves the Negro in his place, but his place is at the back door." When once asked how he and his supporters might keep Black people away from the polls, he picked up a scrap of paper and wrote a single word on it: "Pistols."

Yet, there is something in the American covenant—in its charter documents and its Jeffersonian ideals—that bends toward freedom. Led by a preacher and a patriot named King, Americans of all races stood up. History vindicated the movement that sought to push us closer to our ideals, to lengthen and strengthen the cords of our democracy, and I now hold the seat—the Senate seat—where Herman E. Talmadge sat.

And that's why I love America. I love America because we always have a path to make it better, to build a more perfect union. It is the place where a kid like me who grew up in public housing, the first college graduate in my family, can now serve as a United States Senator. I had an older father, he was born in 1917; serving in the Army during World War II, he was once asked to give up his seat to a young teenager while wearing his soldier's uniform, they said "making the world safe for democracy." But he was never bitter. By the time I came along, he had already seen the arc of change in our country. He maintained his faith in God, in his family and in the American promise, and he passed that faith on to his children.

My mother grew up in Waycross, Georgia. You know where that is? It's way 'cross Georgia. Like a lot of Black teenagers in the 1950s she spent her summers picking somebody else's tobacco and somebody

"'Your Vote Is Your Voice, and Your Voice Is Your Human Dignity': Senator Reverend Warnock Delivers Urgent Call for Federal Action to Preserve Voting Rights in Georgia, Nationwide During First Senate Floor Speech," March 17, 2021, https://www.warnock.senate.gov/newsroom/press-releases/senator-reverend-warnock-delivers-urgent-call-for-federal-action-to-preserve-voting-rights-in-georgia-nationwide-during-first-senate-floor-speech/.

else's cotton. But because this is America, the 82-year-old hands that used to pick somebody else's cotton went to the polls in January and picked her youngest son to be a United States Senator. Ours is a land where possibility is born of democracy. A vote, a voice, a chance to help determine the direction of the country and one's own destiny within it. Possibility born of democracy.

That's why this past November and January, my mom and other citizens of Georgia grabbed hold of that possibility and turned out in record numbers, 5 million in November, 4.4 million in January. Far more than ever in our state's history. Turnout for a typical runoff doubled. And the people of Georgia sent the state's first African American senator and first Jewish senator, my brother Jon Ossoff, to these hallowed halls.

But then, what happened? Some politicians did not approve of the choice made by the majority of voters in a hard-fought election in which each side got the chance to make its case to the voters. And, rather than adjusting their agenda, rather than changing their message, they are busy trying to change the rules. We are witnessing right now a massive and unabashed assault on voting rights unlike anything we have seen since the Jim Crow era. This is Jim Crow in new clothes.

A vote is a kind of prayer about the world we desire for ourselves and our children.

Since the January election, some 250 voter suppression bills have been introduced by state legislatures all across the country—from Georgia to Arizona, from New Hampshire to Florida. Using the Big Lie of voter fraud as a pretext for voter suppression. The same Big Lie that led to a violent insurrection on this very Capitol—the day after my election. Within 24 hours, we elected Georgia's first African-American and Jewish Senators, hours later the Capitol was assaulted. We see in just a few precious hours the tension very much alive in the soul of America. And the question before all of us at every moment is what will we do to push us in the right direction.

So politicians driven by that big lie aim to severely limit, and in some cases, eliminate automatic and same-day voter registration, mail-in and absentee voting, and early voting and weekend voting. They want to make it easier to purge voters from the voting roll altogether. As a voting rights activist, I've seen up close just how draconian these measures can be. I hail from a state that purged 200,000 voters one Saturday night—in the middle of the night. We know what's happening—some people don't want some people to vote.

I was honored on a few occasions to stand with our hero and my parishioner, John Lewis. I was his pastor, but I'm clear he was my mentor. On more than one occasion we boarded buses together after Sunday Church services as part of our Souls to the Polls program, encouraging the Ebenezer Church family and communities of faith to participate in the democratic process. Now just a few months after Congressman Lewis's death, there are those in the Georgia legislature, some who even dared to praise his name, that are now trying to get rid of Sunday Souls to the Polls, making it a crime for people who pray together to get on a bus together and vote together. I think that's wrong. In fact, I think a vote is a kind of prayer about the world we desire for ourselves and our children. And our prayers are stronger when we pray together.

Your vote is your voice and your voice is your human dignity.

To be sure, we have seen these kinds of voter suppression tactics before. They are a part of a long and shameful history in Georgia and throughout our nation. But refusing to be denied, Georgia citizens and citizens across our country braved the heat and the cold and the rain, some standing in line for 5 hours, 6 hours, 10 hours just to exercise their constitutional right to vote. Young people, old people, sick people, working people, already underpaid, forced to lose wages, to pay a kind of poll tax while standing in line to vote.

And how did some politicians respond? Well, they are trying to make it a crime to give people water and a snack, as they wait in lines that are obviously being made longer by their draconian actions. Think about that. Think about that. They are the ones making the lines longer—through these draconian actions. Then, they want to make it a crime to bring grandma some water as she is waiting in the line they are making longer! Make no mistake. This is democracy in reverse. Rather than voters being able to pick the politicians, the politicians are trying to cherry pick their voters. I say this cannot stand....

Amidst these voter suppression laws and tactics, including partisan and racial gerrymandering, and in a system awash in dark money and the dominance of corporatist interests and politicians who do their bidding, the voices of the American people have been increasingly drowned out and crowded out and squeezed out of their own democracy.... Your vote is your voice and your voice is your human dignity.

...Voting rights used to be a bipartisan issue. The last time the voting rights bill was re-authorized was 2006. George W. Bush was president and it passed its chamber 98-0. But then in 2013, the Supreme Court rejected the successful formula for supervision and pre-clearance, contained in the 1965 Voting Rights Act. They asked Congress to fix it. That was nearly 8 years ago, and the American people are still waiting. Stripped of protections, voters in states with a long history of voting discrimination and voters in many other states have been thrown to the winds.

We Americans have noisy and spirited debates about many things. And we should. That's what it means to live in a free country. But access to the ballot ought to be nonpartisan.... The right to vote is preservative of all other rights. It is not just another issue alongside other issues. It is foundational. It is the reason why any of us has the privilege of standing here in the first place. It is about the covenant we have with one another as an American people. E Pluribus Unum, out of many one. It above all else must be protected....

☆

I know what it's like to have a voice, and also what it's like to feel voiceless. I also know that so many men and women have put their lives on the line for us to be heard. And that opportunity, that fundamental right, is in our ability to exercise our right to vote and to make all of our voices heard.

—Meghan Markle, Duchess of Sussex

I've heard you raise your voices, and I know how powerful they are. Make sure you're ready to use them in our elections this year!

—Taylor Swift, singer, songwriter

Protecting the Sacred Right to Vote for Native Americans—Ben Ray Luján, Sharice Davids, Mary Sattler Peltola, and Tom Cole

Senator Ben Ray Luján represents New Mexico in the U.S. Senate, and Representatives Sharice Davids (Ho-Chunk), Mary Sattler Peltola (Yup'ik), and Tom Cole (Chickasaw) represent Kansas, Alaska, and Oklahoma, respectively, in the U.S. House of Representatives.

Statement in Support of the Native American Voting Rights Act, July 24, 2023

When the U.S. joined the war effort after the attack on Pearl Harbor, thousands of Native Americans walked into recruiting offices to serve a country that had already taken so much from them.

And yet, Native Americans have fought to protect our democratic institutions by serving in the U.S. military at higher rates than any other demographic. These brave men and women were willing to sacrifice their lives despite being denied the most basic rights guaranteed by our Constitution. Until the mid-20th century, this included the right to vote.

World War II veterans were among the first generation of Native Americans to be eligible to vote. However, states denied this right despite their heroic military service and U.S. citizenship. Although the 19th Amendment was ratified in 1920 and the Indian Citizenship Act passed in 1924, finally granting citizenship and the right to vote to Native Americans, states continued to restrict their access to the ballot.

For too long, our democracy has excluded those to whom it owes the most.

In 1948, Miguel Trujillo, Isleta Pueblo, came home from World War II a decorated war hero, but was turned away when he tried to register to vote because he lived on tribal lands and was therefore "an Indian not taxed" (tribal members are indeed taxed). Miguel challenged this injustice in court "in order to bring equality to the Indian people." He won the case and changed state law to secure the right to vote for all Native Americans in New Mexico.

Another World War II veteran, Frank Harrison, Yavapai Nation, won the same right for Native Americans in Arizona. In Alaska,

"Protecting the Sacred Right to Vote for Native Americans," *In the News*, U.S. Representative Sharice Davids, July 24, 2023, https://davids.house.gov/media/in-the-news/protecting-sacred-right-vote-native-americans.

Elizabeth Peratrovich, Tlingit, secured Alaska Natives the right to vote by fighting bravely to pass the Alaska Equal Rights Act in 1945, making it the first anti-discrimination law in the nation.

Despite these victories, Native voters still face obstacles at every turn when attempting to make their voices heard at the ballot box.

Historically, Native voters had to overcome literacy tests, intimidation, and poll taxes when voting. Today, barriers include geographic isolation, non-traditional mailing addresses, lack of broadband, limited transportation, fewer polling and registration sites, scarcity of Native language assistance, and precincts that divide tribal nations. These extraordinary problems confront Native voters every election cycle, which is why Congress must advance legislative solutions....

It is incumbent upon every member of Congress to honor our trust responsibility to tribes and to our Native brothers and sisters, not only for the precious blood they spilled for our democracy, but also for the promises the U.S. has made to tribal nations—promises to safeguard unique protections and their inherent sovereignty under the law.

For too long, our democracy has excluded those to whom it owes the most. As we approach the 100-year anniversary of the Indian Citizenship Act, our country must make an honest effort to hold free and fair elections by ensuring all Americans, including Native Americans, can participate in these elections without obstruction.

☆

We're considered wards of the United States to this day. We are separate sovereigns; we have quote-unquote "benefits." However, a lot of that is dictated by the laws and regulations mandated "for us" by the federal government. Native people should become more involved...now more than ever. We have an obligation to make sure our voices are heard.

—Glennas'ba Augborne, member of the Navajo Nation and election volunteer

We have a dearth of voters who really understand how voting works and how elections work, so that's something that's certainly important for everybody to learn, because we need more voters.

—Nicole Willis, member of the Umatilla tribe and outreach director with Barack Obama and Bernie Sanders

Speak the Truth About History—Kamala Harris

Harris was sworn in as vice president of the United States on January 20, 2021. She made these remarks before a White House meeting on Native American voting rights, July 27, 2021.

I think it is important to always speak the truth about history. So, I will remind us of a few facts: Native Americans were denied the sacred right to vote and faced discrimination and exclusion at the ballot box in the history of the United States. Native Americans were not universally granted U.S. citizenship and the right to vote until 1924.

Even after the Indian Citizenship Act was passed, states still barred Native Americans from voting for decades. Arizona and New Mexico barred Native Americans from voting until 1948—and that was on paper, much less what happened in terms of practice.

Where Native Americans could vote by law—we know that, in many places, Jim-Crow-style policies still prevented or denied meaningful access to the ballot box for our Native American brothers and sisters.

And so these truths must be told. They must be told in the context of agreeing that all people should have their right to vote unencumbered. And that, if we are truly a nation that prioritizes the voice of each person, we must make sure that they have meaningful access to the polls.

☆

The more people we register to vote, the more power we have to send certain people to Congress who represent our interests. Don't listen to the people [who] say, "Oh, your vote doesn't count." It's hugely important.

—Kris Beecher, Native Vote volunteer

Though our dissonance and discord can be disheartening, the right to disagree is actually one we should cherish. It sets us apart from so many other societies around the world—as does the right to vote our feelings, our beliefs, our hopes!

—Oprah Winfrey, television host, producer, actor, and author

"Remarks by Vice President Harris Before a Meeting on Native American Voting Rights," White House, July 27, 2021, https://www.whitehouse.gov/briefing-room/speeches-remarks/2021/07/27/remarks-by-vice-president-harris-before-a-meeting-on-native-american-voting-rights/.

Our Democracy Held—Joseph Biden

Biden was sworn in as the U.S. president on January 20, 2021.

Remarks to Mark One Year Since the January 6th Deadly Assault on the U.S. Capitol, January 6, 2022

. . . One year ago today, in this sacred place, democracy was attacked—simply attacked. The will of the people was under assault. The Constitution—our Constitution—faced the gravest of threats.

Outnumbered and in the face of a brutal attack, the Capitol Police, the D.C. Metropolitan Police Department, the National Guard, and other brave law enforcement officials saved the rule of law.

Our democracy held. We the people endured. And we the people prevailed.

For the first time in our history, a president had not just lost an election, he tried to prevent the peaceful transfer of power as a violent mob breached the Capitol.

But they failed. They failed.

And on this day of remembrance, we must make sure that such an attack never, never happens again.

I'm speaking to you today from Statuary Hall in the United States Capitol. This is where the House of Representatives met for 50 years in the decades leading up to the Civil War. This is—on this floor is where a young congressman of Illinois, Abraham Lincoln, sat at desk 191.

Above him—above us, over that door leading into the Rotunda—is a sculpture depicting Clio, the muse of history. In her hands, an open book in which she records the events taking place in this chamber below.

Clio stood watch over this hall one year ago today, as she has for more than 200 years. She recorded what took place. The real history. The real facts. The real truth. . . .

The Bible tells us that we shall know the truth, and the truth shall make us free. We shall know the truth.

Well, here is the God's truth about January 6th, 2021:

Close your eyes. Go back to that day. What do you see? Rioters rampaging, waving for the first time inside this Capitol a Confederate flag that symbolized the cause to destroy America, to rip us apart.

"Remarks by President Biden to Mark One Year Since the January 6th Deadly Assault on the U.S. Capitol," White House, January 6, 2022, https://www.whitehouse.gov/briefing-room/speeches-remarks/2022/01/06/remarks-by-president-biden-to-mark-one-year-since-the-january-6th-deadly-assault-on-the-u-s-capitol/.

Even during the Civil War, that never, ever happened. But it happened here in 2021.

What else do you see? A mob breaking windows, kicking in doors, breaching the Capitol. American flags on poles being used as weapons, as spears. Fire extinguishers being thrown at the heads of police officers.

A crowd that professes their love for law enforcement assaulted those police officers, dragged them, sprayed them, stomped on them.

Over 140 police officers were injured....

We the people endured.
And we the people prevailed.

We saw it with our own eyes. Rioters menaced these halls, threatening the life of the Speaker of the House, literally erecting gallows to hang the Vice President of the United States of America....

This wasn't a group of tourists. This was an armed insurrection.

They weren't looking to uphold the will of the people. They were looking to deny the will of the people....

We must be absolutely clear about what is true and what is a lie.

And here is the truth: The former president of the United States of America has created and spread a web of lies about the 2020 election. He's done so because he values power over principle, because he sees his own interests as more important than his country's interests and America's interests, and because his bruised ego matters more to him than our democracy or our Constitution.

He can't accept he lost, even though that's what 93 United States senators, his own Attorney General, his own Vice President, governors and state officials in every battleground state have all said: He lost.

That's what 81 million of you did as you voted for a new way forward.

He has done what no president in American history—the history of this country—has ever, ever done: He refused to accept the results of an election and the will of the American people....

And so, at this moment, we must decide: What kind of nation are we going to be?

Are we going to be a nation that accepts political violence as a norm?

Are we going to be a nation where we allow partisan election officials to overturn the legally expressed will of the people?

Are we going to be a nation that lives not by the light of the truth but in the shadow of lies?

We cannot allow ourselves to be that kind of nation. The way forward is to recognize the truth and to live by it. . . .

You can't love your country only when you win.

You can't obey the law only when it's convenient.

You can't be patriotic when you embrace and enable lies.

Those who stormed this Capitol and those who instigated and incited and those who called on them to do so held a dagger at the throat of America—at American democracy.

They didn't come here out of patriotism or principle. They came here in rage—not in service of America, but rather in service of one man. . . .

Our Founding Fathers, as imperfect as they were, set in motion an experiment that changed the world—literally changed the world.

Here in America, the people would rule, power would be transferred peacefully—never at the tip of a spear or the barrel of a gun. . . .

☆

I could never have imagined seeing these things in the greatest democracy in the world. Has ambition so eclipsed principle?
—Mitt Romney, U.S. senator from Utah

Jean-Luc Picard once said that the duty of every Star Fleet officer is to the truth. Whether it's scientific truth, or historical truth, or personal truth. That guiding principle is more important now than ever.
—Trek the Vote, a grassroots movement of *Star Trek* fans volunteering with nonpartisan, pro-democracy groups nationwide

Our Election Systems Are Safe—U.S. Secretaries of Homeland Security

Michael Chertoff, Jeh Johnson, Janet Napolitano, and Tom Ridge, former U.S. secretaries of Homeland Security, issued a joint statement in October 2020 in response to doubts being sown about election results in the leadup to the 2020 presidential election.

Our foreign adversaries want Americans to lose faith in our institutions themselves, to become disenfranchised, angry and divided. Even some in positions of power in this country want you to lose faith in the systems of American democracy. But as both Republican and Democratic former secretaries of Homeland Security, we want the public to maintain justifiable trust in our institutions, because the underlying foundation of our voting systems remains strong and secure.

☆

Americans like to think that we're invulnerable, but we are not. Our systems are not. Our democracy may be resilient, but it is also fragile. And that fragility is what is at stake now.

—Stacey Abrams, lawyer and former Georgia state representative

I'm hopeful that despite all the noise, all the lies, we're going to remember who we are, who we're called to be. Out of this political darkness, I see a great awakening. If you vote, things will get better; it will be a start.

—Barack Obama, former U.S. president

"Our Election Systems Are Safe and Our Democracy Is Strong: Ex-Homeland Security Secretaries," *USA Today*, October 2, 2020, https://www.usatoday.com/story/opinion/2020/10/02/trust-american-elections-bipartisan-homeland-security-secretaries-column/5882493002/.

CHAPTER 7

Educate Yourself, and Vote!

Every election is a conversation about what we care about as a country.
—Mark Zuckerberg, cofounder and CEO, Facebook

The ignorance of one voter in a democracy impairs the security of all.
—John F. Kennedy, former U.S. president

A vote is like a rifle; its usefulness depends upon the character of the user.
—Theodore Roosevelt, former U.S. president

The fact that so many successful politicians are such shameless liars is not only a reflection on them, it is also a reflection on us. When the people want the impossible, only liars can satisfy.
—Thomas Sowell, economist and columnist

We've seen how hard it was for many Americans to obtain the right to vote. Voting in every election is a way we can honor their struggles. It's also a way we can hope to help "right the ship of state" if we feel things are going in the wrong direction—or reaffirm our preference for a candidate who's seeking reelection.

Most people would probably say that their votes align with their values. But to be sure that they do, you may want to double-check that you have an informed perspective on the issues and candidates.

Rooting Out Bias and "Fake News"

With the internet and social media serving up content that is specifically attuned to each individual, it can seem as though each of us has a subscription to our own unique newspaper, with stories that cater to our interests but that other people may never become aware of. As the United States grows ever more politically polarized, clashing perspectives based on personalized media feeds are causing American elections to be more bitterly contested than they have been in many years, perhaps since the Civil War. At the same time, artificial intelligence and "deep fake" technology threaten to make it harder and harder to sort out what is true from what is false.

The following is a sampling of the many resources that can help you to detect bias in news sources and avoid being taken in by "fake news." You can try exploring some of these so that you feel confident that you're making choices in the voting booth that reflect your values.

★ Ad Fontes Media maintains an interactive media bias chart that categorizes media sources by their reliability and degree of political bias (from "most extreme left" to "most extreme right"). https://adfontesmedia.com/interactive-media-bias-chart/

★ AllSides (whose motto is "Don't be fooled by media bias and misinformation") presents news stories from sources that it identifies as being from the political left, center, and right. https://www.allsides.com/unbiased-balanced-news

★ The Center for Media and Public Affairs at George Mason University "conducts scientific studies of the news and entertainment industry." https://cmpa.gmu.edu/

★ The *Columbia Journalism Review* has as its mission to be "the most respected voice on press criticism." https://www.cjr.org/

★ FactCheck.org, a project of the Annenberg Public Policy Center, is "a nonpartisan, nonprofit 'consumer advocate' for voters that aims to reduce the level of deception and confusion in U.S. politics." https://www.factcheck.org/about/our-mission/

★ The *Washington Post* publishes a fact checker on politics with stories aimed at discerning "the truth behind the rhetoric." https://www.washingtonpost.com/politics/fact-checker/

★ Media Bias / Fact Check is "an independent website that has promoted awareness of media bias and misinformation by rating the bias, factual accuracy, and credibility of media sources, large and small." https://mediabiasfactcheck.com/

★ National Public Radio's "On the Media" is another source of press criticism, tackling "sticky issues" with "civility and fairness," "frankness and transparency."
https://www.wnycstudios.org/podcasts/otm

★ Pew Research Center is a nonprofit, nonpartisan, nonadvocacy "fact tank" whose aim is to "generate a foundation of facts that enriches the public dialogue and supports sound decision-making." The "News Habits & Media" page covers journalism. https://www.pewresearch.org/topic/news-habits-media/

★ Politifact is a "nonpartisan fact-checking website to sort out the truth in American politics," featuring a "truth-o-meter" with ratings that range from "true" to "pants on fire."
https://www.politifact.com/

★ Snopes describes itself as "the internet's go-to source for discerning what is true and what is total nonsense." Readers can submit a rumor for fact-checking. https://www.snopes.com/

It's worth the effort to look at the kinds of news stories that other Americans are viewing and to determine what kinds of biases and untruths may be contained in the news stories that you are exposed to. Knowing that you are accessing high-quality information on the issues you care about gives you confidence that you are doing the right thing when you make your choices in the voting booth.

☆

Everyone is entitled to his own opinion, but not to his own facts.
—Daniel Patrick Moynihan, former U.S. senator from New York

We do not say that a man who takes no interest in politics is a man who minds his own business; we say that he has no business here at all.
—Pericles, ancient politician and general

A Prayer Only You Can Make

In the lead-up to an election, candidates and parties bombard us with content designed to set up an emotional reaction, to manipulate us into voting in their favor. But the power of your vote is that it is your own prayer for a better community, a better country, a better world—a prayer that only you can make, based on your own values and the truths you have discovered for yourself.

Voting is a civic sacrament.
—Theodore Hesburgh, Catholic priest and former president of the University of Notre Dame

Somewhere inside of all of us is the power to change the world.
—Roald Dahl, author

Don't boo—vote.
—Barack Obama, former U.S. president